PRETTY GOOD FOR A GIRL

SPORT AND CULTURE SERIES

Toby Miller and M. Ann Hall, Editors

VOLUME 1
PRETTY GOOD FOR A GIRL: AN ATHLETE'S STORY
Leslie Heywood

Leslie Heywood

PRETTY GOOD FOR A GIRL

An Athlete's Story

SPORT AND CULTURE / VOLUME 1

University of Minnesota Press
Minneapolis

Copyright 1998 by Leslie Heywood

Originally published in hardcover by The Free Press, A Division of
Simon & Schuster Inc.

First University of Minnesota Press edition, 2000

Published by the University of Minnesota Press
111 Third Avenue South, Suite 290
Minneapolis, MN 55401–2520
http://www.upress.umn.edu

ISBN 0-8166-3659-1

A Cataloging-in-Publication record for this book is available
from the Library of Congress.

Printed in the United States of America on acid-free paper

The University of Minnesota is an equal-opportunity educator
and employer.

08 07 06 05 04 03 02 01 00   10 9 8 7 6 5 4 3 2 1

Dedication

To Jeanie Zumwalt, who showed the way.

•

To Jeff Niesel and Jen Drake,
Susan Bordo, Liz Rosenberg, and Susan Strehle,
who show me now.

•

To Beth Darnell, Jim Kinkead, Victor Flores,
Ray Díaz, Kenny Smith, Chris Hard,
Teresa Meyer, and Sandy Whiteman,
who were my friends.

•

To Doug Rice, whose language is
everywhere in this book, and
to my editor, Liz Maguire, and my agent, Beth Vesel,
who birthed it.

•

To Jonathan Dryden, who understood what I
was trying to say and helped me revise.

•

To Lucy Sherman, Michael Simon,
Heidi Lloyd, Ben Greenburg, Laura Dohn,
Shelly DeKruyff, Eve Rosenbaum,
Amy Karp, Jody Rosen, Rebecca Cangiano,
Mike Wawrzycki, and Cliff Frisbie,
my contemporary-memoir class
at Binghamton University, Fall '97,
who sweated with me through the final stages,
creative writers whose struggles with their lives,
their thinking, and their prose
helped me with my own.

Contents

Preface to the Paperback Edition

In the three years since I wrote *Pretty Good for a Girl*, the story of my experiences as part of the first generation of female athletes post–Title IX (the education act of 1972 that mandated equal funding for men and women in any educational institution receiving federal dollars), the American cultural landscape has changed unequivocally for the better. While once female athletes were dismissed as "not serious" or "too masculine," or were disparagingly referred to as "dykes," the summer of 1999 found a nation captivated by a women's soccer team—so captivated, in fact, that the covers of *Sports Illustrated*, *Newsweek*, *People*, and *Time* were simultaneously graced by stunning images of the athletes from their Women's World Cup victory. The Saturday afternoon of the match garnered major network coverage and Nielsen ratings higher than those for NBA finals. Those of us unfortunate enough to be watching from home saw the unprecedented spectacle of a sold-out Rose Bowl and a rowdily mixed crowd of all ages, genders, and races, 91,000 strong, giving it up for the girls, screaming their lungs out in support of not football or basketball players but female athletes, *women*.

It was a sight I'd never thought I'd see in my lifetime. And maybe it was this sense of wonder and vindication that explained my tears that afternoon when Briana Scurry's save and Brandi Chastain's final kick changed the history of women's sports—and I believe women's lives in general—forever. Maybe that explained the tears of my neighbor, a sixty-year-old retiree who erupted in jubilation when I saw her a few minutes after the game when we were walking our dogs. "Did you see that?" she yelled to me in joy from the hill above. "Did you see all those people? Cheering for women? Women?! The world will not be able to forget this!"

In the days following the match, news commentators debated the question of whether the support for the Women's World Cup was an anomaly, a one-time success based on clever marketing, or whether it indicated real change in public respect and support for female athletes. In the media hubbub, this debate was part of the radio call-in shows on which I was asked to speak about the implications of the World Cup for the future of women's sports. Some detractors argued that our nation will never (despite the success of the WNBA) support a women's professional league, that women just aren't as interesting players, and that when the American consumer shells out hard-earned dollars for sports entertainment, it will never be for *girls*. I argued otherwise, and the amazingly affirmative calls that followed those of the naysayers indicated that our cultural landscape has in some ways shifted for good.

The attitudes of these radio-show callers marked such a radical departure from similar shows I'd done even two years earlier that I was almost convinced that our time as female athletes has finally arrived. The callers were still all men, but rather than the standard "men are stronger than women" and "women athletes will never be on the same level as men" that characterized the conversations two years earlier, this time the callers chimed a different tune: a soccer dad who called in to testify how wonderful soccer was for his daughters, how it taught them competitiveness, teamwork, and a strong sense of themselves. A diehard sports fan from Georgia who called in to comment that the women's teams at the University of Georgia were uniformly better and more exciting to watch than the men's. A schoolteacher who called in to say how he'd seen sports change and empower his female students' lives, transforming them from shy, withdrawn girls hesitant to take part in group conversations and activities to self-confident speakers who asserted themselves in every context.

Despite a silly media thread that focused on Chastain's victory gesture of stripping off her team jersey and exposing her Nike sports bra (which, the Nike spokesperson was quick to emphasize, was specifically designed as outerwear, *not* lingerie), most of the cultural conversations following the World Cup seemed to reflect nothing short of a new world order (as did the astonishingly inspirational *Newsweek* cover that featured Chastain in all of her muscular glory). So did the plan for Wheaties boxes featuring each of the World Cup starters, the first time soccer players of any gender have been featured. So did the advertisements like the Gatorade spot that featured a competition between Mia Hamm and Michael Jordan in various sports, set to the tune of *Anything You Can Do, I Can Do Better*, which showed Mia getting the best of Michael at practically every turn. Girls and women aren't weak little things anymore, *get it?* This is the age of women's empowerment.

In an inspirational cultural context that seems to headily embrace female athletes and sports, *Pretty Good for a Girl* may seem a historical relic, a chronicle of earlier, less progressive times when good ol' boy coaches and their protégés felt authorized to denigrate female athletes and girls were seen as *just girls*, less valuable and skilled than boys in any context. Times when a woman recognized for intelligence or athletic skills was the exception to her gender, not the rule. In the excitement and media hype that followed the World Cup, I was almost convinced that my experiences were now historical, a part of earlier attitudes and times. It is much more exciting, empowering, much more comforting to believe that everything has changed unequivocally for the best, that the problems I faced had vanished in the wave of rapt faces gathered to cheer the U.S. women's soccer team that hot afternoon in July 1999.

But despite my hope and joy at this latest turn in the history of women's sports, I knew that there was another story that was being forgotten in the glow of the television cameras and pro-girl Gatorade ads and *Newsweek* magazine covers. This is a dangerous forgetting, one that threatens to make all the positive chatter about women's sports into that—just chatter. While sports are indisputably a positive source of strength and self-development for girls, they can accomplish this only if the environment in which female athletes throw their javelins, kick their soccer balls, and swim their fast and furious laps is an environment that respects girls and takes them seriously as athletes.

There are many such environments, but as my own story and the stories of many other athletes show, women sometimes compete under conditions that do not always offer them respect or put them on a level playing field with their male peers. Research shows that problems within athletic culture like sexual harassment, overtraining, eating disorders, and inequitable resources and treatment are still part of the experiences of many women athletes. The U.S. women's soccer team, for instance, receives much less money for its victories than does the men's team, which is ranked much lower and enjoys much less popularity and name recognition. Some coaches still encourage their athletes to lose weight in order to perform better, subjecting them to public taunting about their bodies and appearances. And coaches are still forming unethical sexual relationships with their athletes, turning what is a professional relationship characterized by an unequal distribution of power into an illusion of romance. These are problems we find in many parts of our culture, and the sports arena, rather than functioning as the "safe space" many parents believe that it is, is not exempt from these problems.

In a broader sense, the connection between cultural attitudes toward female athletes and public perceptions about girls and women more generally (and the way these attitudes influence the problems above) makes the question of women in sports so hotly debated and fascinating. Like other serious books about women and sports, *Pretty Good for a Girl* is about much more than the subculture of athletes (who are increasingly becoming icons for the mainstream). As the letters I have received from many nonathletic readers attest, the book speaks to questions close to the hearts of many American girls and women navigating the contradictions that characterize their experiences as females in the late twentieth century, the changes to and repetitions of old habits and roles.

But I can't effectively articulate how *Pretty Good for a Girl* speaks to these larger themes in a detached, academic voice. I've found that my readers' words make the connections much more clearly than I ever could, like these words from the review section on the amazon.com website: "The way that Heywood captures the phenomenon of a body at war with itself, its drive to destroy the self it is simultaneously trying to build up, captures, I think, so many young women's experiences, regardless of whether they are athletes." Or these words, from a girl who posted the following commentary on her website:

> Over the weekend, I read a really terrific book: *Pretty Good for a Girl*, by Leslie Heywood. It's a memoir of her experiences as a high school track star. It's about being a female athlete in the early days of Title IX, about resenting and loving and hating the guys for whom sports are a given, the guys who walk around the weight room like they own the place, like they belong there, because they do. It's about running as

an escape and running as a weapon and running as protection. It's about wanting to be the girl with the most cake: the most special, the most loved, the most admired—the girl who's both beautiful and tough and don't even think of messing with her because you'll lose for sure. It's about manipulative coaches and cruel classmates and deadly standards for body fat and beauty. And it's about sex and bodies and fear and power. At times, it's a very scary story. But it also offers hope and the possibility of learning to live for oneself, despite it all. When you finish reading, you know that women's sports are complicated— there are dangers involved, as well as benefits. But Heywood also reminds us why sports are so important, and why we love them so much. It's a really, really terrific book.

I think Heywood's story touched me so deeply because she reminded me so much of myself at 13. Not because I was any sort of athletic star, but because I shared her contradictory ability to love and hate myself so much at the same time. I, too, was confident in my own power. I was in control, dammit. If anyone tried to hurt me, I'd win in the end—I was convinced of that. No victims here.

But I was also utterly vulnerable: covered in armor, but anyone could touch me. The implications of that contradiction make me cringe. At times it was hard to read Heywood's book. But I'm glad I did, because she helped me look back and finally recognize myself. Her book reintroduced me to the person I was at age 13. And I realize, now, that I do know that person. And I even like her. (http://www.melty.com/yammer/011799.html)

Sitting in front of my computer screen reading this particular response to my book, I found myself crying. The ways this reader *got it* made me feel understood and that my words had done something that mattered. It reconfirmed what I knew from many other responses, which have arrived in the form of letters, e-mails, web postings, faxes, and phone calls: my story is both my own and not my own. In the year since its publication in hardcover, *Pretty Good for a Girl* has provoked a range of reactions, from the adulation of "I want to be you when I grow up" (from an adult woman) to thanks from parents who think the book provides insight and help ("I suggest every father or mother who has a young girl interested in sports read this book. It is apparent everyone can take something away from Leslie's mistakes and triumphs") to the disparagement of a few readers who find the book egotistical, antifeminist, or self-centered. What the latter readers have missed that others have not is the way *Pretty Good for a Girl* is not just one woman's story.

Many readers have interpreted my story, I think rightly, as an example of what can happen to girls in an environment that still does not truly value them as athletes and people, environments still affected by old stereotypes—whether we admit it or not— such as the idea that females are inferior and only valuable for their physical appearances. Many have understood the over-training, the eating disorders, the desperate fixation on winning, the hunger for validation that *Pretty Good for a Girl* narrates as a response to those stereotypes. They have expressed the accurate insight that the narrator's egotism and self-centeredness is one common way girls express the kind of deep insecurity that is a logical response to environments that are hostile to them. Similarly, readers have understood the narrator's nastiness toward other women as the characteristic attempt of a young woman to distance herself from negative female stereotypes so she won't be seen in the same demeaning terms. Though she learns better much later, as a teenager the narrator accepts denigrating definitions of women and tries to prove that she isn't like that by being hostile to other women and trying to prove her superiority over them. Apparently this is a common occurrence, for I have gotten letters from women in graduate school in the sciences and other technical fields who have never been athletes but wrote that the narrator's confused attempt to prove her distance from negative female stereotypes was similar to their own behaviors in environments where, like athletics, women still have to fight to prove they are competent and have much to offer.

But do we still have to fight stereotypes? Aren't we beyond all that now? Aren't women encouraged to become computer scientists and great athletes today? Don't we have girl power? Don't parents now encourage their daughters to achieve just as widely as their sons? On the shiny surface given to us in Polo Sport and Gatorade ads, this would certainly seem to be the case. But research in the growing field of Girl Studies—such as that of Mary Pipher in *Reviving Ophelia*, the response of girls themselves in *Ophelia Speaks*, in the voices of the smart and confident young women in *Adiós, Barbie*—tells a different story. While it is true that the stereotypes I experienced when I was competing have changed in tangible ways—the disparaging "you play like a girl" now made ironic in Nike ads, the assumption that most female athletes are not serious or any good and that women will never compete on the level of men and thus have less right to financial support and resources—those changes are not as widespread as most people think.

The results reported in the Women's Sports Foundation's *Gender Equity Report Card*, for instance, found that even with Title IX's mandate for equal funding, "many colleges and universities are allocating resources and opportunities at a roughly 2-1 ratio between male athletes and female athletes despite the fact that women outnumber men on most campuses." The more recent *Women's Sports Foundation Report: Addressing the Needs of Professional and Amateur Female Athletes* (to which I contributed) found that, based on focus-group interviews with elite athletes in nine different sports, our top women's sports teams (including soccer) still struggle to get basics like insurance, financial support for training and travel, and facilities in which to train. While the superstructure of women's sports has improved in countless ways—better media coverage, more corporate endorsement of top athletes, and the breakdown of old stereotypes—the infrastructure of women's sports remains precarious.

So do the experiences of many athletes involved in high school and intercollegiate sports. Discussions with athletes nationwide show that unethical relationships between coaches and athletes remain a problem, as does the "you are only as good as your last race/game" model of sport that leads many athletes—particularly those who use sport as a way of coping with difficult home lives—to overtrain and suffer long-term health consequences. *Pretty Good for a Girl* serves as an example of these issues. It shows the personal and emotional consequences of what sport sociologists have articulated in more abstract terms for years. The work of M. Ann Hall, Cheryl Cole, Jennifer Hargreaves, Kari Fasting, and others has analyzed the social implications of many aspects of female athleticism. Similarly, the work of Michael Messner, Don Sabo, and others on male athletes provides a framework for understanding the ways female athletes are affected by the same attitudes that men learn: to treat their bodies as machines, to renounce any feminine tendencies lest they be seen as "wussies," to work relentlessly to prove their toughness and worth. Though sport is often cited rightly as a way to boost girls' self-esteem, sport also teaches athletes to develop a sense of self that is inherently precarious, dependent on the athlete's last performance. If you are only as good as or valued for your last performance, your confidence becomes dependent on your ability to compete repeatedly at top levels, which no one can do forever.

Pretty Good for a Girl is also the story of the much-discussed "babe factor" in sports, the controversy surrounding the marketing of female athletes according to their physical appearance rather than their performance. Some feminists, for instance, criticize Brandi Chastain's nude posed-with-a-soccer-ball-for-cover shot in a recent men's magazine, and are critical of the way the "babe factor" (the fact that most of the players were attractive in conventionally feminine ways) contributed to the success of the Women's World Cup. Female athletes, they argue, are still having to rely on their looks rather than their skills to get attention.

Some see the sexualization of women's sport as a betrayal of the benefits sport has to offer girls and women. Joanna Cagan writes in an article for the online magazine *Nerve* (http://www.nerve.com/Cagan/hotMamas.html) that for her, "in a lifetime of fluctuating self-esteem and crippling body image, sports has facilitated the few times when I am too happy and preoccupied to run my normal painful analysis of my body and how it rates on the old sexy-meter that drives Hollywood and New York City . . . If I pick up a glove, a bat, a basketball, I am judged on what I do with them—not, for once, on how I look using them." Cagan sees the media hype related to the 1999 Women's Soccer World Cup as a betrayal of that appearance-exempt space, and writes that "in the end, I was forced to witness one of the painful lessons of high school come true on the world stage: the pretty girls always win."

The athletes themselves, such as soccer player Brandi Chastain and volleyball player Gabrielle Reece, tend to see physical appearance as a marketing asset that is not necessarily gender-specific, pointing to ways the male body has itself become sexualized and commodified in recent media culture and to how male athletes are increasingly valued for aesthetic reasons as well as for their athletic successes. Other feminists have argued that whatever it takes to sell women's sports to the public, once they are sold more girls will benefit. It's a difficult question. Though it draws no conclusions, *Pretty Good for a Girl* is the story of one athlete who grappled with the "babe factor" in terms of both its benefits and its harms.

In some ways I believe that the growing popularity of female athletes marks a new world of opportunities for girls and women. It was a world I longed for in the earlier phase of female athletics that *Pretty Good for a Girl* describes. The benefits of sport I experienced—increased self-esteem and well-being, goal-directed achievement, increased assertiveness are now well-documented and accepted. The reasons why sport has always been a fundamental part of my life—the ways it makes me feel powerful, part of something larger than myself, and that, as a girl, I have the right to take up space—are now part of public lore. Yet the less publicly discussed and less affirmative aspects of sport made clear by sport sociologists are still part of many women's sport experiences. There needs to be more to the sport experience than media hype. If it is truly to be a refuge and place of character-building for our daughters and the generations that follow them, we need to move beyond the "sport is great for girls" model and confront some of the darker realities of the sports world. We need to face those realities with bravery and conviction.

Vestal, New York
August 1999

PRETTY GOOD FOR A GIRL

Prologue:
One of the Guys

"*Amphi's Heywood one of the guys.*" *Leslie Heywood is just "one of the guys" as far as the Amphi High School cross-country team is concerned. The pretty blond, blue-eyed junior is the best runner on the girls' team, but she regularly works out with the boys' team. . . . "I want her to stop thinking like a girl runner," Panther coach Ray Estes said. "Not that I want her to stop being a girl, but because I want her to work and think like an athlete. Right now she's just one of the guys." That doesn't seem to bother Leslie. "They [the boys on the team] help me out a lot," she said. "They always push me." And she pushes the guys, too, says girls' coach Tim Barton. "There's a lot of mutual benefit. If she beats one of the JV runners, then we can rib them and they'll work a little harder." The only place either of the coaches sees a problem is in what Barton calls the team concept. He says that without Heywood working with the girls' team, the other girls don't think they can compete with her. . . .*

We get up at four in the morning, that hour like a held breath just before the densest blackness starts to shift, just before the mourning doves take over that brief space of cool hanging in front of the sun, before it starts burning so tight you can't breathe. It's two hours by pickup to Peña Blanca Lake, somewhere south of Tucson, with those open dirt roads either climbing or swallowed by sand. It's the weekly Saturday morning workout of the 1,000 mile club: me and eight of the cross-country guys, stuffed in the back of an old green truck.

The club is summer habit: starting in June, we log in our miles for a hundred days, ten miles a day until mid-September. Every week we turn in our mileage sheets, trying to peer over each other's shoulders without being seen. How many miles for Victor? And what about Ray? Looks like Mike was slacking off a little bit last week. . . . Whoever has the most miles by September is officially "the man," officially most tough. It is a distinction I covet with the fierceness of a thousand saguaros, with just as many prickling spines.

So at four in the morning I get out of bed and drag up my father, who, it must be said, does support me, his four-thirty stagger jumbled by too much night-before beer, the frantic grog for coffee and ten miles in the white Toyota pickup the last thing he would have chosen to do had I not given him something on the level of the high-achieving son, the one who does his old man proud, shining him up in deflected glory in a way that the morning teapot did not. It is this, I am sure, that gets him up, sets the teakettle boiling its whistling stove to bubble through Maxwell House instant coffee, enough caffeine for the miles logged in before the radio is anything but static. *(We want to congratulate Leslie Heywood, ASDM Director of Development John Heywood's fifteen-year-old daughter, on her first-place finish last week in the 8.3 mile Saguaro National Monument Run. John must be very proud of her. . . .)* He's a track dad, you know, the one who always buys me the newest model of Nike or Saucony shoes even when Mother protests, track dad at a time when Nike Air wasn't there and the Pegasus was nowhere near a hundred dollars. So instead it is he who gives me my Adi-Star spikes by Adidas, size six, two sizes too small, the size I insist on so my feet will look like what I think are girl's feet, two sizes too small and close to a hundred dollars, reflecting my status on the track.

But that's by day. He's also the track dad who gets drunk at night and at these times is certain I'm just some whore, prowling the cactuside with too many hills and too many young studs who are boyfriends, yelling at me, telling me this, but really he hasn't hit me for years. The track dad who by day takes me to any practice, even those four-thirty miserable stints, who is at every meet with that same camera that takes the same shot from too far away so I am just an empty figure running around and around the same space in the same way forever and ever and ever. Track dad who wants me to be a boy more than he wants to live. My mother tells me I train too hard and I hate her for this. My dad asks me what year I'll shoot for the Olympics, probably '84, and no one is more certain that I'll make it.

Well, I'd disappoint him, but that was later on. In that summer of 1980, that first wonderful summer of Peña Blanca Lake, I'm hell-bent to beat anything that stands in my way, especially "the guys." There is never a time that I'm not at war, and this Saturday morning is it, all out, for blood and guts and glory, my legs hitting the ground like steel pistons, so hard, so fast, the rushing of blood that rises to my face brightly red. The road is old, riveted by rain run and sand but I fly so fast I hardly touch it. Whatever saguaros fly past by my side, what water-starved ocotillos, looking so dead but so strangely alive, I don't notice. I'm too busy holding my place. I am carving it out, running myself from shadow to guts with every carnivorous stride. I am someone you just have to see, not some soft frill girl invisible from the street. I have muscle, God damn it, have legs, and they are going to have to take notice. Those hunched backs before me, male runners in my way, in front of me wiping me out, turning me to smiles and dust. From silhouette to speed, from speed to a certain sense of place, a sense of my muscle so hard I am sure I am there. Certain; not like all those times I'm not, those times I'm invisible, disappeared from space.

July the 4th, a picnic, my father turning the meat on the grill, my mother serving garbanzos and peas on the redwood table under the birches. A sticky calm, glint of fireflies, hint of the frogs warming up. Then the turn like a yawning mouth had swallowed table, hot dogs, our fingers and toes. My father, a focused blankness all through his face, a resurrection, the picnic table on its end. Dogs drawing away before their ribs were kicked, the slink of their backs, pressed ears. Catsup soaring red arcs through mosquito-thick space, the charcoal making light, still burning before it hit the ground. My mother's face, a handprint as big as a burn.

There is no way I'm going to get burned. I've proved it already, too much before, I'm not the one they can char up. I'm going for them, heading in for the kill, my nostrils curled for it, my lips pulled back in a gasp and a snarl. There is no way they're going to get me, they are mine, their legs like so many matchstick backs, their lungs collapsing as I blow on by, burning myself through the ozone with the fierceness of ciga-rette-holes.

I mark them, fiercely, one by one. A group of them are gone at the beginning, the more casual guys who get through the run by enduring and just kicking back. Not me. This is life, and death, and everything in between. Not for a minute will I let them forget, not for a minute will they fail to see me. We've been out five miles, maybe halfway through. Four of them straggle on behind, three up ahead: is it Mike? Victor? Possibly Joe? It is Ray I catch first; he is smaller, determined but happy to take what he gets—no problem. I open my legs up a little, pump my arms up, breathe deeper down into my lungs. Not just a girl I'm all tough joints with legs and lungs like pumps of lead. The girl who's one of the guys always wins. She's got to win.

A "girl": small, quiet, discreet. Mild and meek. Who smiles, who smiles, who smiles, who smiles. *(Leslie [Airhead], Good luck in your meet today, I hope that you're not in a bad mood. Smile, you're very pretty when you smile. Love, Armando).*

Delicate. Effeminate. Weak. No way. I'll be a monster any day. One of the guys. Invincible. Tough. Like last year: *Yesterday's hot weather got the blame for some closer than expected results in high school cross-country meets. . . . However, the heat didn't seem to bother Amphi's Leslie Heywood. She broke Lisa Otte's course record and became the first runner under fifteen minutes on Saguaro's 2.25 mile course at Pantano Stables. Heywood was timed at 14:51, knocking thirteen seconds off Otte's record. Otte was almost a minute behind Heywood in third place. . . .*

I say nothing as I fly by Ray, feeling larger, more solid at every turn. Victor next. Some practices, not many, I can get him. He is tough. I can only get him when he doesn't really try, but I always mark him. It is a matter of pride. I fix my eyes on his shoulders, a little tight. He isn't running loose today, says he hasn't had very much sleep. Why not, I wonder, as I take in the way his hamstrings angle the ground, too tight, his back too rigid, stiff. Today, he is mine, I can't let him off the hook. I'll wait for a hill, my strength. On the straight stretches I'm a little flat, the power in my legs not much to my advantage. It's on the hills that I can kill, my pistons, steel. I work on these in the weight room, ten sets of knee extensions every day. Every day. My legs are big in the world. When I punch them they don't give. And when I urge them on, like now, heading into that hill, they respond. Big bites, big bites, tearing the road, swallowing the distance between me and Victor like a string.

A string of steel stretched between our shoulders, relentless, pull up, pull tight; devouring the ground, I'm closing in, my lungs raspy as a cactus and twice as barbed. *If I had a woman's body, I'd be afraid to hit. Afraid to move around, lash out. Eyes would slide over me, seeing nothing except maybe sex. When I spoke I wouldn't draw myself up. I'd never stride through any space like it was mine. I'd sit quite still, and I wouldn't say no. A body has to be before it can refuse, you've got to be joined to it.* I'm not going to let anyone forget what I am, someone you don't mess with.

I'm gaining. He hears my footsteps leaving that black map that might just ride him over. He moves his head slightly, a downward tip of the left ear, an acknowledgement that he has heard. He lifts his shoulders, straightens out his stride: the battle lines are drawn. Too bad for him we're heading for a hill. And there is nobody, nothing, that can stop me then. He tries. But his strides are like a spinning top: I breeze by. I am enormous, all open space and closed-out lines, some perfect, flawless, inevitable thing, silent, silent, whisper-thin as I charge into the morning sun with no male backs before me, and six or seven twisted, chastened, diminished forms left struggling for breath in my wake.

Later, though, when the miles have been run, when we pull up dusty, thirsty, tired, ready for food and Gatorade and paddleboats on Peña Blanca Lake, my solid steel has softened. I've picked a new swimsuit just for this, a day in the sun with the all-male team. Now, my hill-domination firmly in place, I can be a girl, maybe it is evened out. If I beat them, they can't erase me. Will pay attention to me, what else—my body is steel but it's pretty, I know from all those guys who keep telling me to smile and following me around. So I play those smiles, muscular fierce in one minute, Barbie blond in the next, my swimsuit black laced with rusty musk and turquoise blue. I get up on the high rock to practice diving, standing just long enough so everyone can look, profile knife-clean to the sky, hair tied back like Bo Derek's.

I hope my waterproof mascara and water shining on my cheekbones will hold, my tanned skin dripping wet. I shine my attention on my fellow runners one at a time, and each basks in that sun until I switch to the next. The others smile together, shout "das!" their code word for disappearance. My body, face, a perplexing, intoxicating miracle: I can make them disappear like I've been disappeared myself. This is another way I can *be*, test my bite, feel alive.

Still, it makes me jittery. Running, you did it; when you won then you won. This is different. I'm playing around—just what is it? How do you win? Smile, well, you have to smile. And giggle, too, like you've not much to say, fluffed like your hair, hot-rollered high. Curled so tight it survives practice, the suicide sweat of mile eight. I guess I do it all right. They say I do, but something is off, a bit out of kilter, too much *(You can be very sweet sometimes but most of the time you can be a real tiger. . . . Hank Floyd—Yo, Les, one foxy chick, that's also a darn good runner. . . . Keep out of trouble, Anthony Perez— You're very pretty and you should be proud of it. I really enjoyed knowing you and especially having a locker next to Leslie Heywood the track star. . . . Love, Troy—I'm going to write something different because I'm not going to write the same thing everyone else did. You are so lucky to be going with such a swell guy. Not really. I'm just kidding. Vince is OK but you're the best and will always be. I hope you train well and come back as next year's state champion because that's what I'm going to try to be. When you do become state champ I won't be surprised. Since you're such a sweet and attractive superstar . . . do well and stay out of trouble. Love, Kenny Smith).* The pretty track star, smiling and staying out of trouble. Next year's state champ. A real tiger. I was a big girl, a Barbie with a bite.

PART ONE

The Practice Field

There are places that are part of you long after you leave them, that live inside you like a certain kind of Friday night. Where the very best part of you dances and jibes, those times you slide all pumped with blood and tongues and twitched alive, you inside this place and it inside you as easy as you breathe. A year goes by, then ten, and still it shimmies inside you like nothing has ever changed, like you've never lived beyond it. Tucson, Arizona is this place for me, a football field ringed by a track, an Eegee's right across the street, a Jiffy Lube practically in the school's back yard, with mountains flanking three sides like a quiet face.

Tucson is a mix of many things, influenced by Mexico, directly south, mythologies of Native Americans and the Old West, and promises of luxury, a better life, that makes it possible to see a street vendor selling tamales on the same corner as a restaurant that sells dinners at a hundred dollars a plate. In 1979, when my family arrived, it was still a quiet town but getting big enough to feel a little bold. It had swollen with an influx of IBMers from Colorado, who came with money and settled the town farther east. Big enough to have an attitude, to mark a place on the map, Tucson was still small enough to have desert spaces where local teenagers could build bonfires in the sand and see possibility for their lives rising up in those flames: the parked stars, the stretching space that for miles and miles was rock and saguaro and sand. For a long time, before it was developed, the best place to go was Rancho Sin Vacas, down Skyline a little farther west. But that was before the security gates, before Skyline Drive was split. Anything could happen here, and did.

In 1979, if you moved to Tucson and had a little money and middle-class leanings and still believed in the American dream and that there was a right place to be and that good people lived in some places and scary people you should avoid lived in others, you moved to the foothills. Somewhere off Skyline Drive, then the farthest artery north, where Swan Road and Campbell dead-end roughly three miles apart. At Swan and Skyline the artist DeGrazia, with his modern-art renditions of Native Americans, kept a studio you could tour at your leisure for a five-dollar fee, and from there a few roads wound right to the base of the mountains above it. White and tan houses of adobe and glass lay hushed in the heat, their closed faces looking out onto streets with names like Pontatoc Road and Hacienda del Sol, Calle La Cima and Via Entrada.

River Road, the dividing line, clearly marked the outs from the ins. North, white families with money, little trouble. South, little money, more trouble. At least that's what people always said. If you lived north of River Road, you had a house, not an apartment. A sizable yard, looking up to the mountains, and certainly your own pool.

When we moved to Tucson from Colorado in 1979, my father wasn't with IBM, but we moved to the foothills anyway, 6601 Pontatoc Road. There weren't enough kids for the foothills to have its own high school yet, only a junior high, Orange Grove, off Campbell and Skyline to the west. Without our own high school, foothills kids had a choice: Canyon del Oro, to the north and the west, known for Mormons and high SAT scores; Amphitheater, to the south and slightly west, known for great athletic programs; and Tucson High, farther south and right near the University, known for its gifted-student program and proximity to the barrio and gangs. It wasn't much of a choice for me. By that time I was fifteen, and running was sharp in my life like the best kind of nicotine high, though because I took it so seriously I never smoked. I went to Amphi.

Tucson, unlike Phoenix a hundred miles to the north, is in an intermediate desert zone, which means it misses the radical swings of the high desert. The days of killing frost are few, with a yearly average of twenty-two, and summers tend not to go as high as the high desert averages of 115 degrees. Oleanders flower outside the windows from May to December, and pyracantha bushes grow bright like flames with flowers every few months.

If you've never been there and are used to any landscape that has lots of green, Tucson is frightening and dusty and ugly at first. Saguaros stand like giants, their crooked arms jutted in warning. There isn't even much picturesque sand, red or tan as in some deserts, and on some days, the endless sky won't do anything but make your throat tight. But it grows on you, those tight throats. If you stay there long enough, you will start to notice little things, the way stony apricots become smooth, edible fruit by June, the way the oleanders hold onto their thick shiny leaves all twelve months. That the cactuses will shoot out bright bursts of color that back East you only see in turning leaves, a color that means death back there and months and months of gray. You can count on the landscape of the desert, which stays mostly the same from day to day, month to month. No surprises, little fear. Each time I go back, the light looks exactly the same.

Sometimes it seems as if everything that was important to me happened right in this place: the northwest side of the Amphi High campus, where, the second year I was there, the weight room got moved to the space where it still sits, underneath the eaves of the stadium bleachers. You could drive right up to the door then, turning left from Prince Road through a chain-link gate, and crunch through the gravel a few hundred feet, park under the stadium's shade.

When I drive by fifteen years later, that gate has become part of a wall. Like a fortress, you can't get to it from that side or any other. So I drive to the entrance off Oracle Road, and, when that entrance ends at a padlocked gate, I park in the alley next to an air conditioning repair shop and a car painter's.

I can't get to the track by foot either. I don't know what I plan to do if I can—lie on my back in the grass on the football field, where I had spent so many hours stretching? Take a few laps for posterity's sake? Sit in the bleachers, watching the ghost of myself fifteen years earlier float her legs around the turns, not a body near her? Listen to the echoes of the crowd's shouts? My coaches' voices?

August: it's hot, the northwest sky threatening rain. The kind of gathered heat I remember well, pressing down around you like walls closing in. Behind the alley there is a patch of dirt, some straggling weeds. Most of the fence—ten-foot chain link—has plastic strips woven into it so you can't see inside. But there is an empty patch over on the southernmost wing, a gap of just a few feet. My fingers on the wire, I look in.

The football field and track are deserted, but other than that they are just as I remember them, sitting solid in the jumped-up sun, AMPHI PANTHERS in thick white letters across the building, now used for storage, on the stadium's south side. School started this week. To the right side of me, on the football practice fields, making me afraid I will be spotted, Vern Friedli and his boys are hard at work, exactly the same as they have been every August day for the last twenty-two years. "Set . . . hut!" rings out in timely intervals, and you can hear shoulder pads crash in the sweaty heat. Vern and two other coaches are there, same as they were in 1980, '81, and '82, the years I shared the heat and wet with just these sounds, meeting for cross-country practice on the same fields with football players who looked an awful lot like these. But fifteen years ago there would have been one other coach. This is what makes me nervous, for the fact that he isn't there has more than a little to do with me.

He used to coach the JV football team and the guy sprinters in track. He didn't usually coach girls. For years after I ran with him, I would see men like him in other places, a certain look in their eyes that can stop you in your tracks. Physically he looked like Anthony Geary, who played Luke Spencer on *General Hospital,* but his attitude was more like Marlon Brando's in *Apocalypse Now:* Colonel Kurtz informing us the world's a petty place. Kurtz with the whisper of a maudlin twist.

He had his own way of doing things, of getting teams to win. It was the way he stood, the way he looked at you as if he could, with a wave of his hand or a single word, decide whether you were worth taking up the space in front of him. He gave his words only to the ones he thought deserved them. If you weren't on top of your game at all times—on top as he defined it—that was it.

A single dismissive look from him could send an athlete out to no man's land, a place where you were beneath consideration or even speech. Years later, reading an essay on Mexican culture by Octavio Paz, I read what seemed an exact description of what Coach Luke did: *When we say* 'Vete a la chingada,' *we send a person to a distant place. Distant, vague, and indeterminate. To the country of broken and worn-out things.* To the country of broken and worn-out things. If anyone could send you there, it was Coach Luke.

These looks—and athletes' fears of them—made his teams

click. He was known as much for his ability to get his guys to perform as for his ready temper, and he was thin like a wire stretched tight. His most familiar expression was a lip twisted a little bit up to the right, as if he was always getting ready to say something sarcastic and laugh at you. The other coaches, the school administration, were careful not to cross him. His athletes worked like dogs for him. To them, every word he said seemed an insight into the secrets of things behind the daily burning of the sun. It was the tone in his voice, the ready sarcasm on his lips that made Coach Luke seem as if he were on the other side of the sun itself, that he had walked right on through and survived it and was challenging you to buck up enough guts to do the same. His athletes gave everything to him and tried. A lot of the sprinters played football, too, and trained with Coach Luke all the way from their freshman through their senior years.

Did the football coaches, barking out their drills across the street, still talk about him? Question his methods? Would they remember my face or the rumors attached to it? Just wondering makes me nervous and shy. I feel heat in my cheeks and imagine all sorts of eyes on me, like I've been caught doing something. They are about 300 yards away and busy, and I am alone in an alley, my fingers hooked to a chain-link fence. Probably they won't remember, or my face has changed too much to be recognizable as *that girl, remember, that one?* I've got a few deep lines on my forehead now, and back then, though I was muscular for a runner and Vern watched me lift many a weight, my biceps and shoulders were not built up like they are now. The football coaches stand shoulder to shoulder, and their bodies, along with the players waiting on the side, form a closed line. They don't seem to miss him.

I stand at the fence outside the track for a long time. The guys on the football team continue to smack up against each other in the sweaty heat, and not one of the coaches seems to notice me. There aren't many people left around here who would remember, but three who would are standing 300 yards away, yelling out censures and encouragements.

My Guys

Summer 1980: the gates have opened and I am in. It's just me and them, Victor, Ray, Joe, Mike, Kenny, Jim, my closest friends. The cross-country guys. My guys.

By high school standards, the cross-country guys are athletes, but not in a boy-enough way, not football, basketball, or even wrestling. Cross-county is for geeks, long gangly misfits on spidery legs. The kind who do debate team or wood shop in their spare time. They adopt me like I am some precious prize. They love me.

I worry about it still, these first victims of my prima donna terror, the guys who take me everywhere I need to go, my faithful companions on nights without dates—these cross-country guys, my dearest friends, to whom I do wrong in a thousand and forty-one ways.

When most guys look at me they don't see me. They see some blank girl instead, some *chick,* and they either ignore me or flirt with me. It makes me want to wear a sign, draw a black line down my face, maybe. Most of the time, if they really talk to me, I'm not just a blank anymore, but how many of them ever do that? The ones that do get some idea, but not enough, never enough of what is going through my head when I stand trying to smile at them and make it seem like it's all right that they're talking to me as if I'm just *some girl.*

The distance guys are different. They take the time to think about the space between what I look like and the things I say. They let me talk, say things that are safe to say only with them. They know what I am before I do.

What my boyfriends don't know, the distance guys do. They have a way of looking at the way things work—ironic, challenging—that's different from anything I've ever known except in books. They take me to drive-in movies with stars like Bruce Lee, with fierce names like *Enter the Dragon.* To the art theater for *Apocalypse Now.* Talk about books by Thomas Pynchon, Joseph Conrad, Hermann Hesse. They drag me to *The Rocky Horror Picture Show* on many a slowed-down weekend night; once Chris stands inside holding my head while I throw up on his shoes, too much dark beer for even my guyness to hold. They spend three years teaching me there is another world I can belong to, when otherwise I would have accepted the starring role of standard blond who goes to movies like *Rocky* or *Friday the 13th* with the football player boyfriend she's supposed to see. I do very little for the distance guys in return. Do they feel graced by my presence, as I sometimes think? They know better, more than several steps ahead of me in this.

Thanks mostly to our coach this year, Ray Estes, racially the distance guys are a mixed bag. Long before I know anything about politics or racial pride, I know he loves his runners. And that his generosity extends to the whole misfit lot of us, all of whom, for one reason or another, fall somewhere short of Amphi's standards for social limelight or easy grace. Victor and Ray because they are Mexican-American. Kenny because he is black. Me because I am (half of me) a loud-mouthed girl who'd just as soon hit you as take any shit. Mike and Cam and Chuck and Jim because they are skinny and brainy.

The distance guys, and me with them, mix up the rules, Coach Estes creating an off-center space where as a pack we find belonging. They are guys my regular boyfriends look down on, low on the social totem pole, partly because some of them live on the south side of River Road, the divide between the barrio and the foothills. Victor, Kenny, Mike, and Ray are on one side, and Jim, Chris, Cam, Charles and myself are on the other. Joe lives too far west to be either.

The nonfoothills side are the better runners. But once high school is over we play right along the usual lines. The non-foothills bunch gets the athletic scholarships to the local community college. The foothills crowd gets academic scholarships to good universities. And I get an athletic scholarship to the local university, known more at the time for its sports than its academics. Who is it again that is tracked to industrial arts instead of physics, English rather than math? It's way too predictable, really.

Fall of 1980, the guys cross-country team throws a surprise birthday party for me in the old weight room on the south side of the track, on a Wednesday night right after practice. Lit up and shining, all I can think is: no one else's birthday has been celebrated like this. There is a cake with a frosted runner on it, carved up with my name. There are flowers, balloons, and a present I will hold onto for years after. It makes me certain they understand everything about me and that, unlike anyone else, they love me. I wear that jacket before and after every meet, a symbol, at least to me, of how much I mean to them. It is a gray and navy running suit of the best high-tech fabric, the most beautiful thing I've ever seen, the hottest thing in running gear before Nike had marketed even so much as a sneaker. I've been coveting something like it for a long time, and I know what it costs. I find out later that though everyone chipped in, it is Kenny who paid for most of it.

In my scrapbook, sitting on the main bookcase in the living room above the TV, there's a Polaroid of Victor and me in the stands before some meet, our backs against the concrete. His shoulders are straight and his eyes are dead on, challenging the camera to speak, the uncombed shock of his black, black hair like an exclamation point over mine. I am snuggled up against him, my head cocked to the side to touch his, my shoulder bending in, my knee up against his. Though he is not smiling at all, I am doing a bit of a simper, giving the camera red eyes. I'm trying to be; Victor *is*. Though he's my friend he's a bit reserved, doesn't treat my every smile at him as if it were some valuable present he doesn't deserve. He knows that it comes with some strings. In my senior yearbook he gives me just what I deserve, writing over a picture of him leading a race:

Leslie, I've know you all these years and you still don't really realize that I am more than a stupid Mexican. It has still been fun knowing you and I hope to see you in the future. Victor Flores. Victor Flores, who knows who he is.

Much more than I know. I do see him years later, but only once: on campus, on the steps of the student union under the marquee of the theater. He is running at the community college, he says, and my voice is falsely upbeat as I say, "Oh, that's great," and ask him how he is doing, skimming over the long lines of so much we need to say that we never say. He shrugs. I'm being blond and superficial in that little-girl way I always get when I'm uncomfortable, hoping to charm. Victor isn't charmed. He always knows better.

Ray, on the other hand, doesn't seem to. I still have the jewelry box he made me in woodshop, nice and big, with my name in black curlicues carved into the top. The workmanship is flawless, the wood unblemished, smooth. I've got it on my dresser like a testament to better times, times when I was really loved, times when the world was mine. Ray made me feel that way. My old scrapbook is filled with the dried bodies of flowers he sent me before meets every week, forever wishing me luck, flowers before every football or basketball game I ever cheered. No one else, not my boyfriends, not my "secret pal" on the football team whose locker it was my job to decorate for a week, gives me flowers like Ray. Those years, wherever I go, there Ray is. On the way to the track. Jockeying for position beside me in the van. He is responsible for those Bruce Lee movies in the drive-in, where he fights hard to sit beside me. The last time I see him, he bails me out once again. Freshman year of college I burn up the engine of my Volkswagen Bug driving home from a trip to Phoenix, and Ray is the only one I know to call, though I haven't seen him in months. I don't see him again after that.

But the one who bears the full-on brunt of me is Jim. There is a 5×7 picture in the paper of us running in the fall of 1981, under the article that previews the state cross-country meet. The article is focused on me, and the headline reads, AMPHI RUNNER CAN WIN THEM ALL. Like they've done before, the camera guys show up at practice and follow me around, hoping to get a good shot. I hate the one they come up with, because it makes my legs look too fat, my breasts too big, while Jim is laughing and skinny, each of his legs clearly defined. He gets some shit from the other guys: there's Jim tagging along with Leslie again. When will you ever learn, they kid him, rolling their eyes. And they are right: he is there for me. I take full advantage. I am friends with him for four years, the longest of any of my high school friends, except for Beth. Three years of high school and one in college, when his father buys him his own little house near the university and I go over to help him pick out furnishings for it: a lamp, some dishes, and plates.

Those plates are the last of him, because sometime that first semester of college, it occurs to me that I am winning races for Division I and Jim is just a student. Just like that, I stop returning his calls. The moment I decide to do this we're in my car and he is waxing ecstatic over the Neil Young eight-track I have just picked up from the discount store for a dollar,

American Stars in Bars. The tape happens to have the track that is our favorite, "Like a Hurricane," which we think of in some unspoken way as our song.

It is understood that I am the hurricane, and the longing that's cutting Young's voice up is Jim's longing for me. Because I won't let him love me, not a bit. Jim, who runs with me most practices in high school, the days we aren't racing, just to talk. Who before I have a car gives me rides from place to place to place every day, sometimes going way out of his way. Jim, who is my closest friend that terrible summer when I need a friend probably more than I need to run, a summer when my mind is soothed by driving all over town with him, delivering meals-on-wheels. Jim, who listens like your girlfriends are supposed to—listens to tales of boyfriends who are doing me wrong, the boyfriend he painfully wants to be and I know it. I drag him through the last inch of it, test his loyalties day after day. I know how painful that is. I know he is in love with me. I count on it. I use it.

By the end of senior year Jim is the witness to a thousand catastrophes, working me through them seriously one by one. At the end of senior year, this is what he says: *Dear Leslie, You know I have trouble writing these things. I hate trying to put on paper something which is better spoken. You already know more about me than anybody else ever has but if you want me to repeat it I will. I care more about you than anybody and love you dearly. If you go someplace other than the U of A next year, I don't know what I'll do. I'll miss you very much. Still I wish you luck and hope you do get the chance to run in*

Oregon. I can't express how much I truly admire your feats in running. By running myself I've realized what you've accomplished. The amazing thing to me is that your tremendous potential has remained mostly untapped. I love you more now than I ever have and will continue to do so as long as it suits you. Please let's stay friends forever. Love, Jim Kinkead. But I do not stay his friend forever.

I don't stay anyone's friend. A different group rules Amphi High, and I need to be part of it.

S a t e l l i t e

Amphitheater High School belongs to the sprinters, and to
their coach, Coach Luke. The sprinters have pumped-up muscles, nicely feathered hair, standard handsome faces, butts that
do much for their Levi's or the bright green running shorts we
have to wear for every meet. Nice legs, nice chests, and they
always run with their shirts off. Walk their lettermen jackets
through the halls, all that. What is known from the female side
as a catch, a privilege to snag them, to walk arm in arm with
them a gift.

I am no gift. According to some of the sprinters, I am trouble. I yell too much. Stand out. I've dated a couple of them,
and I've seemed to cross over some lines. Hank and a football
player named Armando, until I finally settle on Vince. Vince
has a broad smile and a soft voice, a guy who almost in spite
of himself just happens to be sprinter-like too. Gentle hands.
Perfectly feathered hair that isn't ever out of place, medium
bod and a really sweet butt.

The sprinters own the weight room. The distance guys go in

there with me, but they're really out of place. They're skinny and can't lift very much weight. Vince, like all the rest of the sprinters, can do lunges with a barbell stretched across his shoulders at 120 pounds; it brings out those thick rounds of hamstrings that bunch like a fist when he sprints. And if he can do 120, I've got to try it, too.

I'm not allowed to talk to any sprinters in the weight room while they're doing their sets. I'm the only girl in there, with the distance guys—no one worries about them—and the coaches, all men, always watch me to make sure I'm not distracting their guys, baseball, football, basketball, track. Sometimes, without looking, I can feel eyes cutting up on the tightness of my legs, my chest, so my skin burns a little bit red, but I learn early on to forget it and work. I work harder than anyone, the missing link between sprinters and distance runners, who are mostly fairly weak. The coaches don't like this. They look at me and the distance guys, the heavy plates on my bars and frown, but there's not a damn thing any one of them can say. Legally they have to let girls in here, and I lift what I lift. I can lunge Vince's 120, too, as long as someone, usually Victor or Jim, places it across my shoulders so I don't have to throw it up over my head myself. Small under hulking iron plates, each lunge of the hamstring makes me larger, cutting up space. It's mine. I belong here. I always feel taller when I'm done.

I think I settle on Vince because of his eyes, which are very kind, always warm, not glinty like other sprinters. Christmas 1981, Vince and I stand in front of a blinking tree. I've got on a red velour shirt, hair curled up around my face. I'm holding a huge stuffed bear, red bow around his neck, his nose at my ear and big bear butt coming down to below my knees. Vince is holding me, one arm around my back and his other hand on the bear's left front foot. Vince's leg, substantial, nice, a muscular thigh tight in his pants, which run slim up his hip. White button-down shirt, the collar unbuttoned quite low, a V-necked lamb's wool pullover. Smiling and looking down. I look like someone who's been told she's a sweet, sweet thing. The Christmas lights spread over me, blinking. I have a boyfriend who has given me a bear.

But the bear is a rare moment of peace. I date Vince but hang with Kenny. Hang with the cross-country guys, not good, my white hair bouncing around in the midst of their pack, a pack I should not run with, according to the rules, either in practice or out of it. In the unspoken code that says if I date a sprinter I must only have eyes for them, I've transgressed a thousand times. I belong to Vince but snuggle with Kenny in the van or the pickup to and from the trails we run for practice. In his arms, smiling up. He makes me warm and laugh. I light up around him much as he does around me. We get lost on purpose on our morning runs, down some sidelong woods trail, in between silent groves of trees where not another foot turns over the leaves. We run, but we turn to each other, stop, too. Do we ever kiss? He has braces. I think we do, especially one Saturday on Mt. Lemmon, cool six a.m. air, calling birds and ferns and pines, endorphins from running the six-mile hill all mixed with the elixir of each other, arm to arm, mouth to mouth, sweat to sweat. Thinking his mouth the whole way up the hill. Lying in his arms the way home in the van most mornings, the other guys giving us a little quiet, space. They're all in my camp like the sprinters are not, for sprinters have boys in their camp and girls are just for one thing.

The sprinters shake their heads at me when I run by, say *trouble,* and Vince gets smaller and shrugs, "She's OK." And they jeer a little, call him by his nickname, "Lonzo," and give him a series of shoves. In this world, a football field ringed by this, our track, where we spend all our afternoon hours, the sprinters are big and I am a girl, not so big. Except when I win races, which somehow lets me grow. Then I'm big. But off the track, tucked under their arms, I am a shadow, a slow blow job in the desert, the back of a pickup weekend nights.

One day in early spring, I'm in the weight room. I'm sixteen, still the only girl in the place, again with my guys, the distance runners. Not the sprinters, who wear the flare of their hamstrings and biceps like some general's certificate that says the bench press and the squat racks belong to them. Rebel Barbie and her scarecrows carry not so much weight, we win races sometimes, but come on, men are men. There is only one incline bench and we are on it, pumping out sets and fair reps. A couple of sprinters start to circle in, drawing up their shoulders, flexing their pecs, and when that doesn't force us to give over our place, roll their eyes like they are saying, "little wimps." I look at them and snarl. I might be one of the guys with the long-distance men but to the sprinters we're nobody, just sawdust taking up some space. Invisible again. It won't happen.

The guys look over at me as I jump onto the bench, not even waiting to size up the right notches on the bar to place my fingers. I throw the weight up, quick and pissed. With twenty-fives on each side and the bar forty-five, at ninety-five it isn't much, but it is more than any girl in the school can do, and I am sure I belong on that bench. Six reps, seven, even ten, I'm into it cold, I'm not stopping, my face going red and my pecs beginning to sweat. I can feel Jim shift, kind of clearing his throat, and I throw in another couple, racking the weight with a clash.

I sit up and there he is: the sprinters' coach. He looks just like—*just like*—Luke Spencer on *General Hospital,* and this is Luke Spencer's year. A few months from now he will rape Laura then marry her, and the whole country will tune in, whether they usually watch the soaps or not, the hype in the papers approaching that reserved for Prince Charles and Princess Di, whose wedding will also happen that month. Like Luke on TV., Coach Luke is gaunt and thin, skin really white, with unruly threads of albino-red hair fanning the air behind him, thinning a bit right on top. He moves quickly, and is sarcastic a lot like he's sarcastic right now, twisting that smile that says he knows it all and knows it right, your place in the universe nothing like his. I look up at him, ready for a fight. He looks at me like you'd look at a rooster who's strutting his stuff just before he's going to get cooked. Not this rooster, mister, not me. I look at him with his own look that says you don't even exist and you'd better get out of my way. His mouth turns up at one corner and he laughs, "Hey, my guys need this bench and you all should go do something else." I don't move.

Ray looks at me, "Come on, Leslie." I sit. Coach Luke laughs again, turns away.

I'm really pissed now and this weight bench has never seen quite so much fervor and my voice rings out like nothing anyone would question: "Get me the thirty-fives." I throw off the twenty-fives like they were dimes. I've never done 115 but it's going up now, six times, eight times, I don't even falter until ten. I expand like I'm big enough to take on the whole gym and sit up like there's no way anyone could challenge my place. Jim and Ray are really nervous, say under their breaths, "Come on, let's go," but I ask for it, let him turn around, let him just come back here one more time.

Sure enough he does and he isn't laughing this time. He's got the voice of a parent who's been challenged. He draws himself to his rough six-foot height and thunders, "I told you my guys need this bench!" My ears sing and my face is hot and I place my feet as solid as I can and throw out some words like this gym's never heard. The clanging weights and the humming voices all stop. My words hang in the air like they're suspended, like time wound down: "Just what makes you think that your guys," I hiss, "have any more right to use this bench,"— now I'm pounding it—"than we do? Why do you think this?"

I look at him, and first his eyes are quiet, kind of narrow, sitting toward the back of his head. Then they get brighter, as if in disbelief. As the voices stop and everyone listens he starts to move, in what seems like slow motion at first, but then he's on me in a second, so quickly I don't even have a chance to breathe. His white fingers are around my wrist and his face is an advanced shade of red. He jerks me off the bench so hard I think for a minute I'm flying, but then my head hits the wall behind me. I stand there, dazed, but his hands are on my hands again and I'm outside before I know it, backed up against the aluminum siding of that football-player gym, glowering like the bad girl whose father's yelling right up in her face.

His voice goes on and on and the words are like ice or the sound of faraway blows and I can just feel the echo as it rides off my skin and I have no idea what he is saying. I just know that it's all I can do to keep from screaming, that he's trying to tell me that I'm a ghost and he lives, and there's no way I'm going to take this. So he goes on and I don't flinch and he keeps going until suddenly he's back inside and the sound of the weights start to clang like shots and I get the hell out and run home.

That Smell

I have crossed the wrong person, wrong side of the line. Right after the weight room incident it begins: my ugliness seeping up to the outside. They have found me out sure enough, I am not loved. I used to pass through senior hall to admiring stares, whistles that gave me a charge. I loved striding the halls between classes, chin out, shoulders back, my athlete's muscles pumping. I start to walk head down, arms tight. The looks aren't so nice. I walk by, they stop talking. Mark my steps. My shoulders hunch in; I fight not to throw the covers of *Algebra II* like a hail deflector over my face. Then it starts, sharp, a whistle, low, a wall of whispers like a rumble, the dancing of tree branches before the monsoon hits: *You bitch. You bitch. You whore.* Was I hearing things? No. *Bitch. You bitch. Whore. You whore.* And a kind of jeering, not words exactly, but a hiss. Minutes underwater, minutes on hold, voices getting foggy and dull. I bite the side of my cheek to fight tears. I am visible, all right, the stares flinty, corners of people's mouths turned down. I lower my head, charge through, but the hissing grows. The space closes, locks me out. I make it to my English class, where even there I am fixed with eyes and eyes of dead stares. Draw into myself small and tight.

But practice is much worse. It's track season, and I train for shorter distances than most of the guys, so a lot of days I do intervals by myself. Repeat 200s, 400s, some half-miles, sometimes miles. The second hundred meters of the track is the backstretch, where usually no people go. I round it, floating open air, bodiless space. The 300 meters takes me by the hurdlers, though. I tense—the last stretch belongs to the sprinters. I try to stay out of their way. One day they gather just as I am coming around, hurdlers, sprinters, they move in a group. I feel them fixed on me like the headlights of a truck, its engine revving up. Paranoid, I'm being paranoid. This has nothing to do with me. They head for the backstretch together as I charge to the homestretch and around the curve for the start of another lap. I round the curve into the homestretch, safe. But by now they've reached the other side, stand in a line facing the track. *Nothing to do with me.* I'll have to go by them again. I take the corner, muscles flexed, legs extended, lungs tight.

The track spans the football field; along the backstretch are benches where the visiting team sits, its players waiting to get on the field. They head for these, and as I come up on them, they all stand, in a perfect line, facing me. A terrifying mechanical line, beefed up buns and flashy pecs, they turn their backs to me. In unison, sit. I can't hear anything. I feel myself slipping away as I round the corner, my footfalls fainter and more faint. My flying feet don't make a noise, my breath is silent.

When they start songs about me on the track bus I shrink, but I am also getting angry. Singing about me in terrible rhymes all the way to the meets. I grow harder. Lifting weights harder, running harder, my lungs and legs are very strong. I get out there and win. And on that track I am a blister, streak, every stride a stroke that shows them. *Here I am. You can't erase me. Whatever else you want to say I win these races.* I run and run with their hate to my back, and I am racking up all the state's best times. When I finish a race I am not smiling, but snarling, curling my lip a little, and sweeping past their chicken struts and their pushed-out chests like I'm one of them. But every night afterward I am sick. All those nights in April I can't sleep. Like nights when I was a kid, I try to make myself into leather. Pretend I have another skin. I don't. I try.

When dead mice start to arrive in my mail box at home, I know who it is. Construction barricades in the driveway when I get up for my morning run. I put them aside, but they come back. Then FOR SALE signs planted in the front lawn. Then construction barricades *and* FOR SALE signs. Then screaming wheels at midnight, more and more dead mice. Yellow police tape spanning the trees, DO NOT CROSS. At five, my morning runs are so quiet you can hear quails turning around in the brush, no breeze to rattle any leaves. In shadowy spots at the bases of hills, where the moon fades off into clumps of rock, I start to look behind me. I can almost hear footsteps fading back from my sight, tracking my progress down the street.

My parents are fearful of having a daughter so marked. Having our house stick out in the calm neighborhood line, like ashes placed over the door. Because of me, my sex and speed and sweat, my ready words, because I will not smile. Marked. What have I done, they keep asking. And what can I tell them, say?

It's my own fault, after all. I knew what I was doing. I grew too much, "bigger than my britches," like my family always tells me *(that's right, I'm stepping out. Got a 225 squat now. Just watch my butt grow)*. I got fed up with rules at the dinner table, a *good girl* keeps her elbows off the table and takes smaller bites, fed up with sprinters and Saturday night movies and cramped fumbling in old white pickups. I needed more space.

I noticed this swimmer, the smart guy in my history class. We started flirting. He lit way up when I walked in the room, not like Vince, who was half lit up, half holding back, so he could still be a sprinter, big. With Brian I could stretch way out there, larger than life, so I broke all the codes and dumped Vince. Right about the same time as the weight room thing, right before everyone started looking at me funny. Maybe that's why they're doing it.

Now I feel myself marked everywhere, except with Brian. I do no wrong there. He keeps me steady, holds my hand, and looks at me like I am a bright blue robin's egg to him. This year I've been a cheerleader, in this high school hierarchy one step down from songleader. I can't dance, my moves more an athlete's, stiff, so I'd been happy with this. But now, egged on by the names and the hating, a songleader I must be. Brian's older sister was a songleader. She understands that my needing to make the squad could help him, too, nudging him up in the hierarchy.

She works with me for hours each night, choreographing the routine that will be my revenge: once those guys say you are out then you're out, but it is me who will get back in. Yep, I can dump sprinters for Brian, they'll see. Talk back to Coach Luke over incline benches. Whatever they try, I'll still be accepted, a songleader, top of the crop, they can't erase me. So all of me goes into this prancing and smiling, the twisting of hips and smooth moving, the slide of peach-colored taffeta, tight-bodiced dress, full skirt, sliding smooth to the Charlie Daniels Band, "The South's Gonna Do It."

But tryouts come, and though I think I do the prancing slip and slide pretty well, by that afternoon I have lost my place, and damn if those sprinters aren't right. I am nothing, kicked out of my place, some two-bit whore, too much. Can't smile and flirt like the songleaders, clean. The final judgment: the sprinters have won, and I am wiped off the map of position and place. My skin slips. And the dead mice and FOR SALE signs and the posse of sprinters all turning their backs start whirling up and I start to run, hard and harder up the cliff. Crying, crying, blind. A blue streak. Up the hiking trail at the top of my street, the dangerous topmost stretch. Running, blind.

I pass some hikers on the way up, who, I half notice, look at me as if I am a ghost, but I am going fast now, too fast to greet them or choke back sobs. Running through saguaros, up the cliffs, the rocky hiker's ladder back through the overpass into the hills. I hear feet everywhere, blood rushing my head, a tight blur that might burn through space. I am dangerously close to the edges, too near the top, but I am crying so hard I can't see. I'm headed for that rock at the very top, the rock where no trails lead. I get there. And I sit and sit and sit, thinking I should throw myself off. *Monster, awful, nobody, whore.*

Back in my place. No place. *In love with anything to do with men and wild: like a monster, my mother says. A monster in paradise, monster in hell. Back then we lived in a redwood house, rising out of the stones like part of the earth itself. Surrounded on one side by fields wet with timothy, buttercups, cows with tails that slowly twitched, on the second side by pines and maples, birch and oak, layered over each other so thick the sun barely made it through the leaves. On the third side a brook, then a pond full of frogs. Apple trees a hundred yards down the lane, apples mixed with lilacs, raspberry patches with blackberries, sharp green tomatoes, fresh corn. Outside, my place. Chickadees, salamanders, frogs, and in the pastures, many deer. Red-headed woodpeckers and old Native American arrowheads, mud thick like clay on the pond's bottom. Grass and vines and innumerable ferns, a heavy quiet among the trees. All this was mine, and then that house, perfect.*

We were four miles from the closest neighbors. No voices. No cars. Not a sound. When my sister and I would shout in the back, our voices were absorbed by the trees. The loudest sound was the cows and the different combinations of the birds. But at night we longed for other voices. Someone to hear. To come in and say, what are you doing there, buddy, I think you'd best stop.

My father drank Budweiser in cans. Red, white, and blue, clink clink. The sound of the can collapsing, the air whooshing out, the clink as it hit others in the bright green plastic pail. And then my father's voice all right, zipping around like a flame. All that redwood, glass. A long time ago my mother made me a dragon, yellow corduroy with green-felt scales and a red pipe-cleaner mouth. He didn't have wings but I knew he could fly anyway. I used to think my mother made me that dragon so I could fly. I don't think that anymore.

Dragon, they said I yell too much. Once I walked around for a week with a black eye, and no one said a word about it, as if I had somehow done it to myself. I never looked them in the eyes. Outside there were all these spaces, hills, just waiting, when I found it so difficult to sit. Always bursting my skin, like somebody had given me a body two sizes too small, like the Grinch's shrunken heart that eventually bursts out of its frame. And I was bursting. Monster girl, too big for her britches. Way too big.

Dead at the bottom of a cliff, up high enough where no one reaches. In five minutes I will do it, jump. But first let me think. Remember, breathe. Kenny and the green, green light beneath those trees, our arms quiet. With Jim, with Ray, with Mike, with Joe, laughing in the backyard after *Benny Hill,* far-off lights flickering in the pool and all of us plotting the next season. The races I've won and the crowds there, all rooting for me, their voices rising like lights. The way strangers call out my name, stop me in the street to wish me luck.

And Beth, my best girlfriend at Amphi. Beth lives in a magic world, her house the only place except the track I feel at home. Her house is full of constant motion, she and her four sisters laughing, singing, joking, eating. They are like a private art troupe: Regina playing the piano in the living room while strains of Beth's cello and Angela's and Mari's violins can be heard from different parts of the house. Or any of them might be practicing a scene from the campus musical, the starring parts, or scales for a choir concert.

Unlike my boyfriends, Beth doesn't think it's strange I get excited when I talk about books, the way the words in *Wuthering Heights* are like the whispering of my blood. We sit on the floor in her back room by the bougainvillea, bright pinks and bright greens, and after she shows me her paintings I read her pages I've written. Beth is the only one I can talk to about the way the world flattens out sometimes, the gray in my bones like a November freeze back East. And I know better than anyone about the boyfriend she's had since junior high, who plays the drums in a band and wants to take her to *Rust Never Sleeps* instead of the prom, the way she feels late at night on one of those days he tells her she is a distraction from his band and he needs more time away from her to jam with his mates.

For Beth and books and mourning doves in morning and the feel of my legs on the road, the sun on my back, for the air in my lungs as I head up the hill, I want to stay here and remember. I'm not doing anything yet.

Five more minutes.

The last time I thought about something like this was just

before we moved from Colorado and I couldn't see Arizona as anything but death. So one night I listened to Fleetwood Mac's "The Chain" and lost myself in the wail and the jangle of building guitars and somewhere in that climbing took a bottle of aspirin mixed with a quart of Jack Daniels and 7 up. I lay down on my bed, which was just a mattress, to wait. Crickets outside on a cool summer night, through the open window I could hear the dogs pacing outside, the clinking of their collars. Then, I thought they were the only thing I would miss. I had an old white bookcase and a makeshift desk made out of a door painted white. I kept staring at the bookcase, *Big Red* and *The Black Stallion* and *The Crooked Little Path*, *Old Yeller*, *The Incredible Journey*, *Harriet the Spy*. My ears started ringing and I shot out a little, as if my body was far away. And I was Harriet no longer, too old for stallions and dogs. I turned on the radio, and listened to the voices of Lynyrd Skynyrd, that spooky song about the smells of drinking and smells of death, which seemed like fate, this song at just this moment, their voices drifting like I was drifting and I could see my death all coming up voices, a dance of bones like Halloween cardboard tossed around by an outside wind and my head was spinning and ringing and that was it.

Of course I turned out OK. My mother told me she drove me to the hospital, making a wrong turn and doing ninety the wrong way on a one-way street. I told everyone that she came downstairs to get something from my bathroom, found the empty aspirin bottle and panicked, gathered me up in her arms and rushed me out to her Volkswagen Bug. She said I dragged myself upstairs, into her bedroom, and woke her asking for help. But I didn't want to remember my cowardice that way. I wanted to remember the spooky voices, smells, drifting away with them, altogether more dramatic, like my life was worth more if someone had actually come down to my room, put their arms around me, picked me up and rushed to save me.

Five more minutes.

No. I won't go. I'll save myself this time. They can't take me down, not like this. *"Why do you always take everything so seriously?"* guys always ask me. *"You have such a pretty smile."* Well, maybe I do. I can smile. To hell with the sprinters; most of them are graduating anyway. I draw in some air and stand. Come down to face them, fight the silence and name-calling, the blackballing on the bus and in the hall. I get up to leave, pick my way down the trail, steep. My foot catches the edge of a rock just right. I feel my other foot pulled under. My grip is gone and I am falling after all, the edges of the desert tearing at my skin. The rocks grab at me, all those spines, swiping, swiping, as I hurtle down. I black out.

Electric Fence

I wake in the hospital two days later, struggling and shouting about missing practice and that I have to go right away. I
am in a room full of flowers and my head feels like a lead pipe,
my skull a dull thud. There is a woman in white, kind of nervous, standing at the corner of a bed that has metal arms to
prop me up. Tubes everywhere, IVs. I look. Feel impatient.
"Practice," I say. "I've got to go." The woman looks grave,
like someone about to be hit by a train, holds an arm up as if
to say, "Stop!" I start to move but am stopped by a pain that
feels like the shock of an electric fence. "No," she says. "You
can't run." Who is she kidding? I don't listen to her flying
words—"basal skull fractures" and "vertebrae chips, internal
injury"—glancing off me like so many startled birds. All I can
see are my arms and legs. My skin, when I lift the sheet, is an
endless criss-crossed red. A solid mass of scabs. No skin.

With the state's best times, I miss divisionals and state this
year. Brought in by helicopter, Search and Rescue, I have fall-
en forty feet. There are flowers all around me, stuffed animals,

cards, from almost every runner in the city. And they start to come in, team by team. People shuffling and shy smiles, get well. Everyone from my own team comes but the sprinters, who are silent, not even a card. I hear later they have drawn stick figures pitching off a cliff and hang them on their lockers in senior hall. Vince's mom leaves me a note, though, before they start to let visitors in: *Dear Leslie, Came by to see you but can't come in since I'm not a parent or relative. Everyone at the track meet today was really upset. If there is anything you need (or would like) please call. Hurry up and get better—it is not the same without you. Susan Lorenzi.*

The distance guys are with me all the time, especially Jim, who comes twice a day, before school and again at night. When I'm still knocked out, the distance guys leave notes: *Dear Leslie, We all love you so please hurry and get well. Right now we are all worried sick. Please call right when you're able/allowed. Mike Olson. Leslie, We stopped by to say hello but were not allowed to. We miss you in school and hope you get well soon. I wish I had your skill of writing but instead you'll have to put up with this. We'll keep trying to see you or get your phone number. I can't wait to see you better and everyone I know is concerned and worried. Get well!!! Love, Jim. Heywood, I wish I could see you, but the ogres over here say we may not. I really do miss you now, mostly because I can't talk to you and let me tell you my problems, however small. All my hopes and prayers are with you, so you'll be better. Remember, we still have to learn how to parallel park so you can get your license. Love forever, Greg (squirrel).*

I miss the prom. Brian spends prom night holding my hand through the silver bars of the bed. We tell black humor jokes about cliff diving and missing skin. I can almost turn over to face him. I get headlines in the paper, HEYWOOD OUT OF INTENSIVE CARE (Six years later, my first day of graduate school and teaching, a student in the back puts his hand up and asks, "Ms. Heywood? Aren't you that runner who fell off the cliff?" "Yes, I am the runner who fell off the cliff. Your first assignment is . . .") *Heywood, who owns the AAA South's best times in the 800 and the 1,500, suffered a skull fracture and chipped several vertebrae and will probably miss the rest of the season. . . .*

I do miss it. But nothing's going to take me out. I make the end-of-the-season invitational meet a little over three weeks later. I know where I am on the track. Sore, covered with scabs, fighting the electric fence, I still win.

But I'm scared to go to campus. It's almost summer when Brian brings me to school the day of registration for next year; the sprinters will be gone, thank God. I have a creeping feeling, though, that it was not just them, not just their loyalty to Vince. No, it wasn't just the dumping of Vince for Brian that was behind the dead mice. I have done something else. Something I can't figure out.

We sign up in the gym for next year's classes, pick up cards from each teacher's desk. Senior year means Honors English and Geometry, which I've already dropped twice. To get to Free Enterprise I have to go past History. History is where *he* is, the Luke Spencer coach. I angle in the opposite direction, behind some bodies, sliding my shoulders to the side.

My hair gives me away. A voice hails me when I'm in the line for English, someone from the social studies side. A sarcastic voice. Coach Luke. Sarcastic myself, my right eyebrow and corner of my mouth twist up. "Leslie. Leslie!" I turn around. "What?" "Ever had American Government?" "Don't need it." "I know. But hey, you missed the state meet." He is watching me, hard, but it doesn't feel like before. This is concerned, kind of friendly. His eyes still laugh, but not quite so sarcastically. "Yeah—so?" "So I'm coaching the AAU. You could make up for it. There's the national meet. And scouts from every college. Want to run?"

I look straight at him. For him, he's being nice. I can feel something from him, teasing, gentle, kind of warm, but each word still takes a little piece of me. Walking anywhere near him feels like you've gone through an X ray and disappeared in the process. His eyes, nothing in them, as if you're not in front of him at all. But now he's smiling. He rakes his eyes up and down me, rough, like guys who want to ask me out always look.

I drop my eyes and mumble, "Those guys." "Leslie, what?" "Those guys. You know. Your sprinters. They'll be out there." Coach Luke laughs. Puts his hand reassuringly over my wrist. He has warm fingers. "Oh, those guys. I can handle them. They do what I say."

My heart's beating now, pounding out the veins along my throat. I draw myself up. I look straight at him. "You'll get them to stop?" "They'll stop." "Then OK, I'll run." "Great.

First practice Friday at seven." He takes his hand from mine, his eyes still on me as I turn, trying not to smile too much. I float away. I'm not a stone. I want to jump up and down, to scream. But there's a twinge in my stomach that spreads through my chest. Maybe. Maybe it's over, the plague, the siege.

Summer Skin

Every night at seven the stadium lights start to come up and the sprinklers spurt at the quick-browning grass. I'm in the middle of repeat 200s by then. The sprinklers by the first turn have half a head, so they soak part of the grass but also the track's first four lanes. Since it's still 103, we don't mind. I'm training with the sprinters—the only other girl is a hurdler's six-foot little sister, who just finished eighth grade. They do what Coach Luke says and leave me alone. One of them—nicknamed Lou, after Lou Ferrigno, the Incredible Hulk—even gives me a grudging "Hi." I smile, really wide, for what feels like the first time in months. My scabs are falling off. I am getting back my skin, and a summer tan covers the scars up.

We run. The sprinklers distract us, maybe take a couple of fractions of seconds off our times, but the shower of water mixed with sweat feels like a sudden contact with cold metal. I finish, hands on my hips, breathing in, cooling down. "Leslie," Coach Luke says, "Run it through here again." "Why should I," I say, "I've done my ladder." "I know. But running through the sprinklers makes your T-shirt wet. A nice sight." "Yeah," I say, "I'm sure it is," and my face gets a little redder, embarrassed, angry, kind of pleased. My stomach twists, and I forget it. I run through the sprinklers, pump out another set of sprints.

Next week, Beth drives me to practice in her white Chevette when she doesn't have cello lessons or rehearsals. I'm done for the night and we sit out on the grass, waiting for the cool that comes as the light falls. "My parents are out of town for a couple days," I say. "I'm going out, won't have to worry about when I get home." "Must be nice," she says, "I've got to be in by ten. I've got musical theater in the morning." She drops me off at Theresa's; we go out for Swenson's and a late movie, one of those early *Friday the 13th*s.

I get home at one and the house is silent; even the dogs are asleep. I sit in the kitchen, drinking Tab. I start to drift, sleep washing me out, gentle cycle. Then I jump: the phone rings. I look at the clock. It's one-thirty. I stare at it, two rings, then four. Like a scream. I start to reach for it, then pull back from five, from six. I pick it up on seven. It's him.

"I heard you talking," he says, "and I know you're alone." He wants to talk to me and come over. "Do you always want to talk to all your athletes in the middle of the night?" is all I can think to say. I feel my heart in my chest, pounding like it does before a race. "No," he says, "I'm reserving that particular pleasure for you, and it's in your best interests and this is why. Remember what those guys did to you last spring?"

His voice is really low but I can hear it there coiled like a spring, there's more to go before it will unwind. I try to act tough but my voice shakes. "Yes." "Well, I got them going. I made sure." "You did?" "Yeah, I did. It's your senior year next year. This year you missed the best meets. You're running great times with me, but you've got to keep it up or the college recruits will never want you."

Will never want you. "I know."

"Well, if you don't let me come over, right now, tonight, I'll set them after you so hard you won't have any idea what happened, and you'll just fuck up your season, no fast times, no recruiters. No one will want you, not even the community college."

"You turn off Skyline Drive," I say. "On Pontatoc. 6601."

Stupid: for years after this I get chills all over and go numb at the sight of a car that looks like his, Ford Fairmount, 1978, a terra-cotta orange almost the color of his hair, with brown stripes like wood-grain along its sides. Sixteen years later I make myself look at his picture in the yearbook to remind me, and all there is is that same sense of a person who is not quite real, someone you knew too well in some past life, maybe, the no, no, that never really could have happened, did not happen, has happened, did.

It is here that I am caught, in the happening. Where memory gets tangled with too many lives. One night, air breathing, life. Desert quiet, so heavy, out. Sun not out then, lying in wait. Hills of extremity, cold stars and deep heat. Plants that need so little water to survive. Balled tight. Once in awhile, a blossom like mist, the next day petals in pieces blanketing the ground. Fierce, they struggle, fighting the sun, which always leaves at night so abruptly, firing orange, tonight. This night, this. One life, one body, one low light in one house among thousands all nesting these hills, protection from the sun. The air still filled with heat hanging low, gathered up, blanketing the rocks. Sand, a blankness that can't reflect. No cicadas yet, they wait for the first hint whisper breathing of light so subtle no one can touch it. No touch. And the quiet like ice, my sister sleeping in the other room (was she really there could she really have been there she must not have been there). The light low, not very sure of itself, waiting to be swallowed up.

I am waiting. I can't see into the next room where the dining room table, glass over teak, sits reflecting slivers of moon from its dull surface. I can't see. So dull. You cannot begin to think how dull *(Oh can you put me to sleep can you rock me to sleep rock me gentle rock me slow don't you know how much I need this, someone to scratch down the sky)* but this is not a place I can survive and need. Remember this is an ordinary table we're talking about. You can get them at Pier 1. So I am not seeing any moon's dull light glinting off the table's surface. I am waiting. My life, some central fight of it, about to begin. I know. I cannot see beyond my hands, the darkness swallowing my feet. Heat and failing light. Heat and falling light.

I'm sixteen, and they say I'm hot, a tease. I must have known this was coming. I sit in the dark, watching the creosote bush compress itself in the still-warm wind. I look at my hands, which seem swollen and big. I can't see my feet. When the door knocks I go to it like I knew this, like this has to happen. He laughs. He starts talking, words, words. I get the whiskey. We sit and drink. Then, out of nowhere, he gets tender. He is saying that his parents are dead and that his father hated him. He is saying that he got revenge, that now everyone listens. He laughs and says his runners do whatever he wants, and I am thinking it will be very soon now very soon and my body will be going away and it is a short time and it is a long time and the sky is gray and I can't feel my hands and my ears are ringing and he is speaking and his voice goes on and it breaks he cries and reaches out he wants me to hold him and like a wooden toy I fold him in my arms and I feel his thin shoulders tremble and I know soon he'll pull himself together by breaking me. He is a ghost I am a ghost and we are floating free and there is no kitchen counter and there is no floor, and I am waiting for him to do it, pick me up, and when he does I only stiffen slightly.

His voice is off-key, something masked. "Which one's your room?" he asks me. The small black gap off the main hall. We walk in. My eyes go right to the beds, awkward teenager twins, sticking out from either side of the orange corner unit. Lumpy, off to the right in the half-slant light, like an unbrushed dog, unloved. My hands are not at this time swinging open the top of it, turning on the stereo inside.

This afternoon—ten hours ago—I was listening to Stevie Nicks. I left her on there. I wonder if she is gathering dust, because I cut to the radio, KLPX. Ten hours ago I lay down, lost in jangling, breathing in, breathing out, before practice and the quarters that would rip me up good.

I'm looking hard at the shape of those beds and I feel Coach Luke's hands on me but all I can think about is Tom Petty and Stevie Nicks—the way their faces look when they play "Insider," their duet. Petty looks straight ahead into nothingness, tough. Stevie looks nowhere else but at him *like my mother used to look at my father right before he'd hit her in the face.* There are thin arms now around my back, and legs against the backs of my knees. So thin, so thin, like wind, a breeze that blows by then quits. Nothing in it.

Too quiet tonight, I've got no rhythm. The bedspreads, which I hate and don't bother to tuck, rub rough against your skin. Yellow-and-white goddamn checks. Both bedspreads are pulled up. I do not tell him which bed. He puts me where I always sleep, and our bodies barely fit. He's under me, so the tops of his feet stick off the end like out of a magician's box; I can just see the feet, a white leg. We don't kiss.

I am thinking hard now, mouths and lips and Stevie Nicks. If I touch him under the arms, along the nipples, maybe he'll lie back into it and won't have to touch me. If I'm down on my knees at the end of the bed and if I use my mouth just right.

But I have no mouth. I am not in my own skin. Looking down, I am watching this other girl in my body, my bed. Smoother than a whisper I'm battened down tight, some steel enclosure sliding into place, my steps echoing like the concrete floor of a meat locker. I know at this moment I have known this girl for a while and I haven't liked her. She got me into this, she. Smiling and flirting too much and too much. Opening. And I am closed like stone. Drawn up. I don't need to feel a thing. She is pitiful *so like my mother*. Just look how hard she's trying. Her face moving over him, the moonlight coming through the acacias by the window outside so that his skin is very white, his legs, like a whippet, tight and thin.

Of course, he gets impatient quite soon with her fumbling, and he pulls her up and then down on her back and she's not even moving very much and I wonder for a second what could be wrong with her. What is wrong with her? He moves very quickly, but she's still. Her face is turned away from him. And I wonder to myself what could she possibly be thinking, who she is. Somewhere toward the end she puts her arms around him, and I watch like a cat until he pulls up his clothes and goes away. I wait for him to go. Just outside of her door he pauses, throws her some words: "See you at practice. Seven p.m."

Yeah, buddy. At seven I'll see you, too. And I know I will be seeing his face everywhere after this. I have marked him. But she's still lying there like the dumb shit that she is and as soon as I hear the front door close I run up to her and pound her still shoulder and say, "Come on come on we need to run."

Inside of this urging to run, I am stunned. When he stood up after, he might not have known he was changed. If I'd been able to look I might have seen that his spirit had lifted. Or that he felt a kind of strength in his hands. Or that he felt drained, like a dying river, the currents too clogged and too thick. I think about his slightness, whisper-thin. I forget to look. A clogged-up artery, building my heart. Which beats. But nothing happens.

Except that everywhere I see his face. Everyone walking

toward me is him. Anyone who touches me is him. And I'm
out of there. It doesn't matter. I quit. Fuck them, I'm untouchable. They will all touch her from this point forward. She's the
one who likes it, not I. I don't have time for that shit. I've got
races to win. She can sit there sniveling and feeling all she
wants, I've got more important things to take care of. Get up,
you stupid bitch. Get up, we have to go. And we do—over to
Beth's house and through her window, where, choking on
words we try to find words to describe this and fail because
she gets choked up she is so weak: Beth thinks I am confused.
Not me. I'm just going to run. That's it. Just run.

So that night we are back out on the track. *She* wonders
what he will say to her but he shows nothing. His face doesn't
move. He is more than stern, like I've done something I've got
to make up for. Flaw in my armor, maybe. "Heywood! Let's
see another two! A little faster—I don't have all night!" I roll
my eyes as I try to catch my breath, *Yeah, I know what you
have time for,* and I wonder as I am running if he is watching
my legs and if the set of my mouth will make his breath catch.
*He must be watching me that certain way, like the sun won't
come up without me behind it.*

But he looks at me no differently than he looks at his sprinters. There is nothing in his eyes. *Well two can play at this one.*
I draw myself up, run hard, and act like I've never seen him off
the track, like everything he says is up for question.

For at least two weeks, he acts like nothing whatever has
happened. Except that a few days later some flowers come, the
card marked NO NAME GIVEN. *She* likes this. Except that he

starts pushing me harder, then harder again. *I like this.* Sprints and sprints and little rest, repeat 800s, 200s, 400s, and every one of them timed, him holding the watch and calmly appraising the shakiness of my legs, yelling "Go! Let's go!" again and again and again. "Good job." "You're two seconds behind on that one—go again."

I run and I run until I can't stand up, and I am proud of this. I can hold up under anything, anything at all—give me some more. More and more, and then I'll do that, too. My lungs are liquid and my legs are rubber, and still I will round out the turns of the track, on time. *See. You can't fuck with me. You thought that you could but just watch me, I can take anything you can dish. Watch me. Just watch. My legs, my pumping arms, the way they curve.* Every instant his eyes are on me I'm alive, and I live for these practices, 103 degree nights, and it is not too long after this I start running the best times of my life.

PART TWO

Desert Heat

It's the Fourth of July again, seems to come round every year with its hints of violence, thick. All those firecrackers, snapping up lives. All those drunks. And I am drunk myself again, with Beth. We are at a downtown Tucson ballroom, hotel, where her boyfriend's band, Electric Freedom, is playing. Beth is not drunk, I never remember her drinking. Her boyfriend's best friend, Bruce, goes with us to the ballroom, and we sit. There is an empty chair to my right, Beth and Bruce on my left. We're talking. And then that emptiness is disturbed, something in it, and I turn. It's Coach Luke.

Beside me, again, laughing at me, again, like he is my fate, like he will just keep popping up everywhere I turn (and isn't that just an excuse? Why didn't you just get up and walk away, you pitiful shit, why do you use this idea of fate to comfort you, why do you make yourself into a victim this way, why aren't you strong enough to resist him?), *and he starts kissing me and Beth and Bruce start laughing, what surely must have been an absurd sight, Coach Luke, intense, his thinning hair of*

*twenty-eight, his mouth covering much of what, if it were vis-
ible, would be a defiantly teenager face, bones closing tight,
kissing back with a fierceness that fights to stand up to his parallel drive that is mounting her, pressing her head back, her
mouth pressing hard back at him so she will not be pressed
back into Beth, ending up in her lap, all this pressing and
pressing in full public view, and then they are gone, and Beth
looks around, not knowing where they went and the teenaged
girl that Beth was watching does not know, either, the whiskey
has taken over and she doesn't remember anything at all
except coming to in his bed on her knees and hearing herself
groan, wondering again how it is she got undressed, how it is
that her body can be doing these things.*

Our track club is called Desert Heat, and our uniforms are
bright red and deep, deep gold, like the sun at noon in its most
sadistic gleams. Red Dolphin shorts and gold singlets, the sun a
jagged-out red cutting the swells of our chests. Desert Heat. I
wonder if he thought of this name, the way it would hiss nice
and tight from the back of his throat when he spoke it; hang
there in the air, its syllables black and sharp and stiff. So all of
us representatives of our grinding desert heat go to the regional
meet in Albuquerque, where Coach Luke drives us in the van.
Me (800 meters and 1,500 meters) and Robin Campell (long
jump, hurdles), Vince Lorenzi (sprints), Matt Dobbins (hurdles),
and Conner Stevens (long jump and sprints). Robin's brother,
Mark (400 meter intermediate hurdles). Kenny Smith (800
meters). I can't remember who else. I giggle with Robin most of
the trip; from the back seat of the van, we harass everyone by

playing Tom Petty and Fleetwood Mac on my old tape recorder over and over, until they plead with us and then bribe us to stop with the promise of extra chicken nuggets at Kentucky Fried Chicken, where we will be stopping to eat. Which works for Robin, but not for me, who never eat anything fried.

I keep hoping Coach Luke will notice that Robin and I keep shouting the lyrics to that Tom Petty song about the woman who's in love but not with him because I have spent the whole trip as a woman in love with Vince, wanting more than anything to get him back. Showing good sense, Vince is ignoring me. Except for Robin, I haven't talked to anyone else, have ignored Coach Luke stone cold. He doesn't like this, keeps trying to talk to me in a soft voice on the field before the races, popping innuendos at me in the middle of conversations with everyone else. I keep rolling my eyes and then walking away, so the guys start looking at him kind of funny.

On the last night of the meet Coach Luke sends Conner to my room to persuade me to meet him by the pool "just to talk." Conner has to talk me into it, his voice soft like the promise of something I'm not supposed to know. I don't remember his words but rather the flatness of his eyes, the look in them so close to Coach Luke's own, and then his mouth, the line of his upper lip, so set it makes me want to chew on it a little. Whatever he says, I do go. Coach Luke is sitting in a chair by the water, soft lights. I stand, watching the water, looking away.

His voice cracks a little bit when he is speaking. "Why have you been avoiding me?" he says. "What's with you? Every time I try to talk to you you walk away, and you've been all over Vince. I thought you guys broke up a couple of months ago." "We did." "So why do you keep hanging around him? Why won't you talk to me?"

My face is hot. I am embarrassed and I shrug. The tone in his voice makes me feel stronger, because it's getting high. He needs something from me. I have the advantage here.

"Leslie." His voice sounds so sad I look up. I look at him. He doesn't look sarcastic, and his eyes are really sad. I don't believe it. "You don't want to do anything but hurt me," I burst out, and he looks sadder. He shakes his head. "No." "Yes. What the hell else would it be?"

"No," he says again. He pauses. He keeps his eyes right on me, and he leans toward me. "It started out like that. It did. I wanted to bring you down, Leslie. I thought I could get those guys to break you, but you didn't break. I had to try. You were so pretty. So sure of yourself. So . . . tough. Not like a girl. But Leslie . . ." His voice trails off, and the way it does is telling me to look at him again, and I do. He doesn't look like he does on the field. His mouth is not sarcastic. "It's not like that now. Not like that at all. I would do anything for you. I don't know what happened. But I love you. I just want to be with you. That's all."

I feel myself swooping out of myself, enormous. *He wants to be with me. He loves me. Love, a cold word. And now I am a cat again, cruel. Can't get to me now, can you? Gotcha where I want you, sweetie. Like my teeth? Like my fist right through your face? And oh will you hold me right next to your chest and stroke my face and tell me that everything, everything will be all right, that you'll hold me forever, keep the ashes away, wipe out the black lines that slash up my face, the grayness that flattens me out? Hold me? Touch my lips over gentle like I am nothing you'd ever blacken, touch. Or throw away* and I am far outside him, soaring huge up and away.

My arms are crossed over my chest and I'm feeling as sarcastic as he ever was. "Love me? Oh, yeah, I like that one. What do you even know about me? Right. Like you wouldn't get in trouble for this? How could we ever do anything together? How much older are you? What would anyone think?"

He's still leaning toward me, his elbows resting on his knees. His hands move quickly as he speaks, and I'm watching them. "None of that matters. I don't care anymore what happens. I don't. I love you too much. I don't care if I lose my job. I don't care. I'll quit. It doesn't matter. I just want you. You. I want to be with you. It's just you."

Just me. Two things are rising in me, one of them dry: *You shouldn't be giving me ground like this. Trying to break me, but it's you who are going to break. Choose your battles more wisely. You picked the wrong tiger, the wrong piece of meat. Didn't you ever look me in the eyes? What you saw there would have stopped you . . .* I start calling him on his clichés. I draw myself up to that meat-locker freeze even though my face is flushed. I say "Well, I don't love you. This is stupid, and you're probably just putting on an act."

I am divided again; that feeling girl is in me. I feel triumphant, she feels tender. She is glad he has said it and wants to say it too. I show no tenderness at all. I've gotten the advantage now, a hold he won't be able to shake. Barbie magic, the kind I still don't understand, but I'm more than glad for it. His contempt, his hate. The great coach, who's got everyone terrified, reduced to pleading by a pool. By me. It took me to get to him, lips and legs, sharp mouth. Let's see just how far I can take it.

"Forget it. You're crazy. I'm in love with Vince," and I look at him like he's a lizard, beneath my contempt, a look I've seen on his face when someone's performance is not up to snuff. I know this is the right move. I go back to my room, face burning with frozen delight. I beat her out, triumphant in this, because she wanted to put her arms around his neck, kiss his face. But I win. Of course I win my races, too, because that is what I do. I run decent times, 2:21 for the 800 and 5:02 for the 1500, and qualify for the national meet, which only Mark and Kenny and I do. The three of us for the next three weeks, training with Coach Luke, flying with him on the plane.

Training up to that meet gets pretty rigid, and the coldness toward Coach Luke isn't something that I can always sustain. I still run with the distance guys on Saturdays, and run my distance miles—at least ten—for the 1,000 mile club in the mornings, but he says that it's wearing me out and I'll have to choose. So I tell him OK but keep running in the morning anyway. My training becomes faster and faster at night, more reps, less rest, faster times. Often I sneak to the side of the track and throw up, though I know his eyes are on me and he sees. Often I am so high from lack of oxygen I get dizzy.

But my whole life depends on this performance, on keeping up, on completing this next quarter on time. I am visible in his eyes, my body fully there on the track, only if I am getting it right. My times start dropping, and I am exceeding every expectation, everything that is asked and then one further. He has not worn me down, and I feel it in his voice, like a shadow starting to creep its way across concrete: a faint hint of respect, like a promise.

RUNNERS 2ND IN NATIONAL MEET *Desert Heat Track Club performers Mark Campbell and Leslie Heywood both took second places in the Athletic Congress national track meet in Lincoln, Neb. . . . Heywood took second place in the 800 in the girls' 16–17 age group, with a time of 2:13. She also made the finals in the 1,500, taking seventh place with a 4:41.*

In a matter of weeks, I have cut eight seconds from my 800 time and twenty-two from the 1,500. This is unthinkable. Nobody improves this fast. Of course I think it is because of him. Of course he says it is because of him. All of this is mixed with talk of love, which makes part of me soft but not the other. Which makes me long for a gentleness in his eyes and those few moments he has touched my face. Then, in an instant, I snap; fuck that, I just want to run faster. We plan how he will train me through cross-country; he even speaks to Coach Estes about this.

Soon after the nationals my parents insist we take a trip up to the White Mountains, where they have rented a cabin. I can think of nothing I'd rather do less. The thought of being locked in a close space with them where maybe I won't be able to shut the door makes me panic, my chest go shallow like I'm out of breath. I can't stand the noise, the anger that jumps out like an assassin from behind every tree. But they say we're going. The four of us in one space. I decide I will escape into the woods with a book and use the time on the drive up there to ride by myself in the bed of the pickup. I'll be away from their words, an acid that dissolves my skin. I've got another world now. I'll think about Coach Luke, the strategy, my next move. Part of me feels like I know I'm supposed to, flattered, full of love. But I know there's no love there. At least not yet.

Late that summer Coach Luke is house-sitting for another coach in the foothills outside town and asks me to come see him. I tell him I will run there, which gives me a good reason to put my twenty miles in. I arrive, twenty miles and barely a sweat. He goes for me right away. But something's wrong in me. There is a click, almost audible, like the electronic window of a car on the driver's side, sliding up into place.

My chest feels like there is a wall inside, and that feeling girl's behind it. Like a statue carved from too-hard wood, I give him a look that makes him stop. My eyes say go away though I am moving toward him. He looks at me. I don't remember what he says, but I know I launched in: he is a miserable excuse for a coach, a human being, twenty-eight and so pathetic, so empty he has to go for sixteen-year-old kids, get power from training his sprinters like thugs.

I go on and on, my words pumping me higher and higher. He is far underneath me, one square backyard plot like the thousands clumped together you see from the windows of a plane. It has happened. I have become untouchable, transcendent, grown to my next incarnation. I have made myself safe; from him and from everyone who will follow.

Circus

That summer part of me is still trying to do what I'm supposed to, love a boy who's good to me, and I have Brian, but
I have split into several pieces by this time. Sitting with him in
the audience high up in the stands on a Saturday night date
night at the Ringling Brothers circus, somewhere between the
tightrope walkers and the elephant trainers, I blurt out that I
have done it, had sex, and that it was with my coach. Brian
looks at me with eyes like those you would shoot at a man
who has murdered a child and asks me how could I how could
I and within an hour is saying that we should do it too to make
it even when before we haven't come close. I get a sick feeling
and I hear that word again running up from under, not spoken
at all but still hanging there, *whore, whore,* and some real
hurt, like *how could you do it not with me* and his eyes have
something missing that I need back and two hours later I am
doing it with him in the cramped back of his Escort, slate blue,
his body on mine like revenge.

We are together off and on for about another year after this.

I've got a lot of pictures his brother took right before Brian left for college in another state. We both want these pictures, but I think me especially: before he leaves, I give him a fistful of envelopes with my address and stamps already on them. In my favorite of these I love the way I look, though it's not so good of him. But I'm perfect: purple polo shirt (that he gave me) open only to just beneath my throat, my hair this soft, bouncy float of blond, blond waves, perfectly in place, drawn back from my face at the top and finished with a white bow, Brian's strong hand resting on my shoulder just underneath my hair. My face is smooth, and I'm smiling, gently, my eyes softened by shadow. I try so hard to be *this*. Simple, uncomplicated, sweet. White like my hair, blank like the smiles I force onto my face. Nice girl. Clean.

In the autumn of that year I am back with the guys' team. I have had enough of it all and don't long for anything but the win. Except the new guy on the cross-country team, thin as a whippet but much cuter. Because he is after me I am after him, too, just to make up for all these hands that have been on me, leaving their prints. The two of us were often together in the paper that fall, along with this picture of me that they ran several times. In it I stretch out in the grass and smile like some unfractured girl, some whole girl, beam out at the world like I have some place in it. Coach Luke tells me about the jokes later, the way the other coaches tease him about what is it that isn't him that's making me so happy in the grass. I just turned sixteen, and they are twenty-eight and thirty, forty and fifty-two, and when he tells me about it it ruins the picture for me.

It makes me feel guilty, like no matter what I manage to look like or do there will be something wrong.

It is then that Beth tells me it is high time I stop. Coach Luke has talked to her, stopped her in the hall at our locker to ask what I am doing, why I will not speak to him. "I don't understand," he says, "she won't talk to me. What's she doing this weekend, do you know? Has she said anything about me?" He has talked to my little sister, too, in class. "Aren't your parents afraid," he has asked her, "that I'm going to do the same thing to you as I did to your sister?" But when I look over my shoulder sometimes after practice, he is watching me. At a football game, I turned around and he was right behind me. At night, I hear scratching sounds outside my window and I imagine it is him.

Beth says it's no good for anyone. She has seen the long looks all over Brian's face, aging him. This is too much, people just don't do this. She tells me at lunch as we are sitting outside on the concrete walkways, our legs dangling over the edge into the grassy court. "You can't," Beth says, "string men along behind you as if they are beads, play with their affections and then throw them away, like one of your trophies, not even like your trophies, more like crushed dirt." *And what is it they would do to me?* Another door slams down, concrete. My eyes flash and I tell her we can't all, you know, be as perfect as she and I am burning and burning and I don't know why and the hum of other voices has stopped and all there is is this white, white rage. I look at her, the fear in her eyes, rich brown in her hair and I know she is right. *But I'm not even sure that the body they touch has anything to do with me, all that I know is that it runs. And I starve it,* making sure it stays hard like the metal on a truck. All I want is to run and to run. Don't you know it? Can't you see it, haven't you heard?

This time the Athletes of the Month are not what you might expect. They are not basketball players . . . they are not even football players . . . Victor Flores and Leslie Heywood are the athletes of the month. . . . As good as Flores is, Leslie Heywood is his equal and more. The Arizona Daily Star *called her "The Triple A-South's premier female cross-country runner." This is only one example of the many times she has been written up in the local papers. . . . Heywood, unlike the other girls on the team, trains with the boys' team and holds her own. . . .*

I am an athlete, I train with the men. I'm not soft, I've got an athlete's thick skin. Don't ask me to smile and simper, don't ask me to open up and let you in. Look at me, I'm not just a girl, I win races, win races, I can think. I'm not giving myself over to some dumb guy. I wouldn't be able to run.

High winds held down most efforts in high school track yesterday, but nothing could stop Amphi's Leslie Heywood, who recorded the state's top times in two events. . . .

If only you could hear the roaring in my dreams, these men spinning all around me who can't turn away I am so big. Every day I grow bigger, like a flame, burning a black hole across space. So they can't forget me, erase me, laugh and turn away, so I won't float alone with nothing whatever to hold. Not feminine. No open airy space to find, a looseness like fucking the void. You'll slam up against me and smash your head. Don't fuck with me. When violets poke their warm heads out of the thickening grass, I smash them. My biceps, brick thighs stand between us. If you touch me, your hands will leave no traces, not even a bruise. Grind me to dust and I'll grind you to dust. As I become sawdust, a tough, stuffed doll.

Untouchable Face

All women are idiots, except for maybe Stevie Nicks. I know my mother is. She stays with my father when I know we should leave, moaning and crying through more than one bruised face about love. Well not me, you Jell-o–breath. You can be mushy, but I won't.

Girls aren't worth any of my energy or time. Silly little things. Not serious. Can't bust a gut for nothing, just earthbound and slow. I won't have anything to do with them. *Take no prisoners* my father always says, and at least he is right about this.

I started giving up on girls in junior high, when I dumped my best friend Maria in order to join the track girls. Even though Maria's pony MJ had taught me speed, I left her for blue and gold uniforms and curling irons and girls with wings. Then student council and cheerleading, not to mention Paul and Jerry and Scott and Eric, who voted me girl with the prettiest eyes. Not for long. That's when my father got another *really good job* and we moved to Arizona. My hard-drinking, authority-hating father, who couldn't bear to stay for more than two years at the same job, answering to the same person. Arizona, another new place, new faces, new kids, and I had to prove myself all over again.

That would be running. I love to run alongside the guys because then I'm worth something. My mother and father, the screaming things that they say about me, don't matter. I have my own world, with the guys.

But this fall I'm not the only girl who's one of the guys. Now there's also Martha: new kid on the block, who runs fast enough that Coach Estes decides she should run with us, taking me down a peg or two in everybody's mind, since now there's another girl, too. But she runs with us only some days. The *really* hard days, it's me and the varsity guys; Martha goes with the JVs. The rest of the girls run together. Any girl with any chance to win races runs with the guys; everyone knows this. But I want to be the only one, JV or otherwise. The only one who's any good. If there's anyone else she makes me smaller, pulling me back. *Girl. Girl. Girl. Girl. Silly. Incompetent. Weak.*

Martha's blond, too, but no one could mistake us. She's taller than me, longer legs, with nowhere near my muscular definition. I think her face looks like a squashed toad, and I tell everyone this in a netted voice. Nowhere near as fast as me or as pretty; why does everyone keep talking about her? Who needs her when there's me? Word's out that I have a sister running this year, a freshman, and at meets everyone looks for her and guesses, because she is blond, that Martha's the one. "How could they think she's my sister when she's so ugly?" I keep saying, loud enough for everyone, including Martha, to hear. It's under my skin like a burr, an ache I just can't make go away. I roll my eyes at the slightest mention of her name, and I walk by her in the locker room as if she were a breeze. *Feel blank, bitch, blank like I know you are.* She tries to talk to me every day, be nice. The sight of her makes me claustrophobic; that she sits in the van with us, that she gets to talk and laugh and joke with us makes every day an all-out war where I prove over and over how insignificant she is just by how far I can beat her. Which is far. It always is.

Any guy who talks to her gets a look meant to blast him away like a *Star Trek* faser, for absolute loyalty is my price. You can't be in her camp and mine, too. It makes the air thick, people quiet. The guys joke less, sit more uneasily in their seats. My flirting with them is tense, because I keep looking at her out of the corner of my eye to make sure she sees just how much I am loved here, that there is no room or need for her. The guys know I am doing this. I don't care. I'll do anything. The only one or nothing—what good is it to be one in a pack of faceless girls, a silhouette with a ponytail, just girls, just girls? Not me.

As if having Martha around isn't bad enough, now there is also my sister, who as a freshman decides that she wants to go out for cross-country too. She doesn't work out with the guys, but I still have to put up with her on my team. Everyone pays attention to her because she is related to me. Watching her, waiting for what they assume will be her natural talent to come out—after all she is my sister, same genes. Same genes but not the drive—I know she doesn't have what it takes. I'm the only one who does, the one with enough blood and guts. Martha, my sister, useless skirts, burrs in my shorts, mosquito bites, a set of terrible itches, a rash spreading over my skin. They become friends. Go everywhere together at meets. Sit by each other on the bus. I try to ignore them. But they're all over my face in my frowning, the stiffness of my back, the way my jaw is set against them.

It gets so how I feel on a given day depends on who has and who hasn't noticed Martha. In the article that previews the cross-country season, which appears the day after my seventeenth birthday, the double columns, placed on the left, run through all the teams and the promising runners. On the right, given just as much space as the writing, is a picture of just me, the one where I'm stretching in the grass, looking up and smiling, my blond-bomber best. OK, the world's in order. But then the story screws it up. *Leslie Heywood, regarded by many coaches as the top runner in the AAA-South, and Martha Compton will provide a one-two punch for the Panthers.* God damn it! I don't want any "ands," or "one-two punches." I want to be there alone, so far ahead I am the only one who gets a mention. Not as a girl, in a category of my own. Not ordinary, nothing, the same old thing who no one takes at all seriously, guilt by association. Damn Martha Compton. I want her to get the hell out of my way. I want to disappear her so I can stand clear and free. She takes away from everything I have worked so hard to do.

But she does anything but disappear. In the dual meets, she

usually finishes behind me—*really far* behind me, but the next runner to finish, nonetheless—the one-two punch. I want to be the one-punch. Dual meets are on Thursdays, so every Friday morning the first thing I do when I get up is get the paper, even before I run. Heart pounding, blood in my temples a bit, scanning fast, looking not for what they say about me but for what they have not said about her. No Martha in this one, great: *Although Amphi's Leslie Heywood took only 12:20 to run the girls' 2.1 mile course, Buena runners placed third through seventh to give the Colts the victory.* Martha finished that race forty-eight seconds behind me. But another paper mentions her: *Heywood, after a near-fatal fall last spring, has come back in winning fashion. In the Junior Olympics, Heywood finished second with a time that broke the standing Arizona girls' high school record in the 800 meters. In the Buena match, Heywood and teammate Martha Compton finished first and second. Heidi Heywood, younger sister of Leslie, finished an impressive seventh.* Teammate, sister of Leslie, begone! But the next week is better: in the column on boys' and girls' cross-country, they do not mention the girls' meets at all, but they run a picture of me, tired and smiling right after my race, with a caption that says SETS RECORD in bold. Who needs to mention any of the other girls? Next week, a mixed bag: I get the headline, HEYWOOD KEEPS WINNING, but they mention Martha again: *Heywood extended her winning streak, taking her fifth consecutive meet victory of the season. Teammate Martha Compton finished second.* And on and on. Everything in me rises up when she is absent,

I feel a grim delight. But the sight of her name, like a very deliberate slight, sends me sinking.

Worse even than the papers is Martha's fixation on Sebastian, the sweet new guy I have marked as mine. Seb also is winning all his races, taking the division by storm. Martha has a crush on him she talks to my sister about. She giggles and whispers in the locker room. And she keeps trying to talk to him with her eyes turned up, even when I'm around. My face turns red when she does this, and I often turn tight on my heel and walk away. He mostly gives her the cold shoulder, but *still*. When she starts wearing her hair the same way as I do, right down to the very ribbons, I'm out for her blood. I don't look at her, speak to her, hope my performances will just erase her.

I jump in glee when Seb goes on record in praise of me. In October, the paper runs a feature, where he says, *"People here are urging me to run, like Leslie Heywood. She runs with the guys and she's incredible."* He sees, and now so does everyone else. They have to see, and then maybe they'll stop talking about Martha as if she were even in my league. The next week, after the state-wide invitational Seb and I both win, they run our pictures side by side. I win the race by seventeen seconds; Martha is seventh, forty-nine seconds behind. I keep very close track of this. The first thing I always do after finishing a race is turn around and stand close to the finish line, so I can hear her time as she comes in. Make sure I'm always cool and rested before she finishes.

A good week is when they don't mention either Martha or my sister, just say *In what has become a weekly routine,*

Amphi's Leslie Heywood set a course record, this time on the Canyon del Oro course. She ran the 4,000 meters in 14:12, breaking by 1:04 the record set by Nina Putzar. Despite Heywood's efforts, CDO defeated the Panthers and Rincon. Whenever someone says the words "for the team," I roll my eyes. I'm glad when they lose and I win. When Martha's left out, I'm much bigger.

I seem absolutely unbeatable for the state championships, not a person—especially Martha—anywhere near me. I win by margins like thirty-nine seconds. Fifty-two. I have a strategy in mind. I'm trying to run like Secretariat. I was nine years old when he won the Belmont Stakes by thirty-one lengths to take the Triple Crown. "The length of a football field. The length of a football field," Pete Axelrod in *Newsweek* kept saying, in a tone of awe, disbelief. I want to be talked about like this.

I followed every Secretariat race, watched his every move. I collected every article and kept them in a thick scrapbook of yellow-gold, the pages neatly labeled. I even wrote stories about him, and, like magic, eight years later, I have become him. His running style is mine: get out front and keep going.

No one could touch him. No one can touch me. The tone of the articles that described him is the same as the ones about me. He was undefeatable, and so am I. We're in a world of our own. Untouchable place, inspiring reverence: GIRLS' CROSS-COUNTRY LED BY HEYWOOD *Heywood won the Tempe Invitational by over seventeen seconds in front of second place* with a time of 13 minutes and 20 seconds over the 2.5 mile course. Heywood has also won every meet that Amphi has participated in this year.

AMPHI'S HEYWOOD LEADS THE WAY FOR GIRL RUNNERS *Leslie Heywood doesn't like to lose. Fortunately for the Amphi High School girls' cross-country team, she didn't do it very often. Heywood dominated the local cross-country scene. . . . the senior has been named Captain of the All-Star Girls' Cross-Country Team. . . . Leslie is a very intense competitor and a very dedicated athlete. She hates to lose and is willing to work hard to make sure she doesn't. . . .*

Untouchable, and yet I do lose. Two days before the meet I start to feel shaky in practice, so dizzy. I think maybe I have not eaten enough, but by nine that night my fever has climbed to 103. I spend the next day sweating and freezing in bed, reading *We the Living,* by Ayn Rand. Which makes me cry for these people, so much like me, struggling to rise and getting pounded. But it seems that maybe I've pounded myself this time. The fever doesn't break, I can't eat anything. State is the next day. I'll do it anyway. And I do. But I am not untouchable. I surge out to the front like I always do, but unlike Secretariat, I just can't hold it. Something collapses inside. Like a meltdown. A top that's stopped spinning, I watch bodies go by me like that one bus you're just not supposed to miss.

I finish seventh, and to make it much worse, unbearable, really, Martha finishes second. There is no way to excuse it: I choked. Nobody knows what to say to me in the van on the way home. I refuse to read the papers. I have lost my place and fallen, hard. Shooting, falling star. Vanished. For the moment, only Martha is big.

I know somewhere Coach Luke is laughing, all the coaches are saying *it serves her right, who the hell did she think she was anyway. Thinks a bit highly of herself, that girl. This should take her down a peg or two . . . we knew she couldn't do it.* I choked. I can just hear all the snarky voices; even the lockers seem to mock me, the jeering faces I am sure I will see if I dare look.

But I don't look. There is only one thing I can do. Shake this flu and turn toward track. My last chance. My very last. And I need a coach.

It's a Girl

I don't want to be anywhere near Coach Luke. I'm scared, because maybe I need him to run fast, but his voice getting soft and all oily makes me run the other way. Coach Estes has told me flatly I am more than he can take. "Why a five miler today?" I am always saying. "Wouldn't it be better if I did eight today and intervals tomorrow in sets of ten?" This is not what he has planned, why this and not that and what about this. And then I'm always getting mad and acting out, he says, terrible to Martha. Accusing him of favoritism. Never, he says, has he seen a runner running so much out of hate. *It will burn you up*, he tells me, *you will get burned. Go to Coach Luke now, I'm through.* So it's Coach Luke or nothing, or the women's coach, Tim Barton. Who, as the women's coach, is a joke—the very bottom of the coach heap, the residue left in the peanut butter jar you don't even bother to scrape out before you toss it. I won't speak to him, either. Senior year, now or never. The papers may love me, but except for Junior Olympics, I haven't really done anything worth mentioning.

I need times the recruiters will notice. I walk around thinking and thinking. Coach Estes refuses, and anyway I'm tired of the way he treats Martha more gently, the way he speaks to me with an edge in his voice like I'm a harassment he just wants to go away. But the idea of Coach Luke gives me a clawing feeling.

It's late fall in Tucson, the sun putting itself away. The few trees that have leaves have lost them. The air's frigid at night, though it is still often hot during the day. After Modern English, my last-period class, I head into the empty locker room and change. The metal clang echoes down the cleaned-out rows. I take off past the graveyard in the park across from campus, throw myself into our eight-mile loop. The air can't make up its mind. It's still hot in places that you pass through like someone's shadow, surrounded by a light coolness that dances off my skin like I haven't got a problem in the world. Arizona sunlight so clear, so sharp, I must be able to think of something. But it's tangled in my head, crisscrossed all over like the cactus my elbow swings into: *So who will coach me? What am I supposed to do?*

I've heard some rumors, about a woman. *A woman.* But word's out that Jeanie's a little different. Everyone knows female coaches are less competent, there for the girls who aren't serious, who are out there for an activity, not to compete. If you want to be any sort of athlete you've got to train with a male coach, the guys. But Jeanie's new this year and everyone says she's totally tough. She's supposed to coach women's soccer and the female sprinters in track. I've seen her on campus: she's maybe five-foot one and has hair almost that

pretty good for a girl

long, which she wears pulled back in a huge ponytail up under her visor. She's compact, muscular but thin, said to have been something of a sprinter herself. She moves quickly, purposefully, like what she's doing has a place. The other women coaches are slower and kind of thick-bodied, and nothing about them stands out. But Jeanie's eyes are focused and intense, and she has a clear, sharp voice that carries. I've seen her talking: she looks straight at you, her speech forceful and brief. As I head into mile five, my strides efficient and clean, it is clear to me: it's got to be Jeanie or nothing. I've got to walk in there and convince her I'm worth working with.

I march into her office, avoiding the other coaches' curious eyes. I introduce myself, but she laughs, she already knows who I am. I tell her I need a coach, although I stumble and am full of vague reasons about why. I do tell her about Coach Estes, how he says I have a temper, and that I tend to question his workouts and he won't talk to me about them; I say I'd rather have someone who would discuss what I do, because by now I know some of the things that work best. She nods and does not turn away at this. I cannot remember much of what we say; I just know she takes me on, a whole other job for which she is not paid. Asks what I have been doing for training, comes up with a program for me on the spot. Agrees to meet me on the track the next day.

We hit the track and talk about the quarters I'll do, the intervals between, and why we are doing them now, at the end of November, what we will use them to build toward as January becomes February becomes March and the season starts. Jeanie's not looking at me like I'm this unpredictable firecracker about to explode in her face, not keeping a physical distance or looking away or mentioning me as an afterthought, like Coach Estes often did. Her attention is all on me. She's also not looking at me as if I'm a primo Corvette, fired-up and ready to ride, the way Coach Luke sometimes did. She's looking at me like someone she can reason with, discuss a game plan, as though I have a level head. I attack the turn on that first quarter feeling that something has shifted. I am physically strong, but durable strong. Serious strong. Not like I'm proving something, but like I'm already there. I *am*. I am running because it is what I do.

I want to please Jeanie, but it's much different from pleasing Coach Luke or other coaches. With them I was convincing them every single day: I am different than other girls, serious, worth something. I know that Jeanie already knows this, it's in herself. The way she walks, the way she looks. The cadences of her words. She is serious, worth something, and I know without her saying it that she wants to give this to me. Not part of her, a power over me, but the two of us struggling for something else. I don't know what we are struggling for, but I feel her there and I feel it in me with the deepest kind of longing. I have never felt anything like this, and it takes me awhile to get used to it.

The Catch

Just before the season starts I get a full-court press from Conner Stevens. He's talked to me a few times in the past fall on behalf of Coach Luke, but the last time he talked to me I felt a shift. A tension, subtle, thick. He was the football quarterback this year, big star. He's trained with Coach Luke since he was a freshman. More than anyone else, he is Coach Luke's boy, and acts it: the guy every girl wants because he goes through us one by one with no more regard than he has for empty beer cans. Each girl thinks she can hook him in, but since he and Vanessa Hewitt split last year, he has not paused for a single one. Not for lack of trying: there are rumors three different girls have slept with him in the same night. A hot thing. But he's got that same cold glint in his eyes I've so often seen in Coach Luke's. His every smile, word, a challenge, a cynicism ready to bite. He asks me pointed questions about Brian. About my training. A slice to his words like he might bite me nice. I give it back to him. We circle. And by January, he lunges in for the kill. I bare my teeth. I bite back.

I don't mean to cheat on Brian. I don't. But the coldness in me rises to the challenge. The most subtle, dangerous kind of fight. I watch his teeth, feel his mouth. On me, hard, long before we ever touch. I know this is wrong, not, my wits tell me, how I should spend my last high school desert spring. But I know he and Coach Luke are setting me up. This only turns me on like a hungry dog, so lean and impossibly mean. Impossible to turn away and I do not turn.

The weekend Jeanie and I are going up to Flagstaff for an indoor meet, he asks me to a party that Friday night. I know what saying yes means. Again, like fate, my parents are going away just this week. They rarely go anywhere, but they have left me this weekend free. I can feel it in me so deep it makes me run my fingers along my teeth. Catch their edges. So. Maybe I can let go for a bit. Break out. I have been training so strictly, disciplining my body piece by every toughened piece. And it's craving. I am running so hard on the track my feet are burning, inside, in the bones, so much I have started to worry. At the end of my quarters my feet are hot. I ignore them, but I am strung tight, and Conner's sprung my trap for a night. Let me out. I come teeth bared and ready for a fight. To mark him.

It's a party at his friends', the Wexlers, these football-playing identical twins who walk by his side like his personal thugs. These guys know how to drink, white-blind like me, whenever I relent enough on my training to do it. The hardest fuel, Everclear, 100 proof, smooth. Conner picks me up in his El Camino, deep blue, polished so the moon is glinting off it. I keep looking at his lips. Pressed together, thin. We don't bother

talking. We get to the house, and I head for the sticky red
Everclear punch. We drink out of stadium cups, a few hours,
cup after cup, talking to his circle of friends. I am talking and
vaguely aware that somewhere he is in the next room and I
feel him pulling me toward him as in a bad cartoon, one of
those traps the Road Runner's laid for Wile E. Coyote,
maybe. Beep beep.

At a certain point he's at my side, his hand on my elbow in
a clench. "Let's go back," he says, gesturing toward some open
door, to a bedroom piled high with jackets. I follow, my hands
running ropes along the back of his jeans, the twin columns of
muscle in his back. The tips of my nails touch skin just above
his belt. He turns. His hand is on my chest and he stretches the
seams of my shirt even though it is hard blue denim, reinforced
with heavy thread. I am white-blind drunk but focus on him
like a top speed quarter I've got to break. We maul for a while
but don't let go yet; too much noise, people drifting in and out,
reaching under us for their coats. "Let's go to your house."
His teeth on my neck, his fingers inside me, tight. Under my
nails bits of his flesh. Again we are silent in his truck but I am
thinking his lips so hard I am biting mine and I am trapping
my hands under my thighs. We go directly to my bedroom,
land on the same yellow-and-white checked spread. But there
is no hesitation at all this time. I am anything but still.

My teeth, his teeth, breaking skin. On top of him, underneath. Not enough room we are on the floor, tear into each
other like meat. On my knees, a slow voice without any
words. He moves up slightly; a flash of pain like the cut of an

axe, a warmth like rushing blood. Hours go by like warm liquid, because light breaks over us, and I start thinking about the bus for Flagstaff and the meet. He says he will take me. Bruised and spent, still biting, we pull apart. He helps me read the map, figure out which bus I should transfer to. He drops me at the station, my Adidas spikes hanging from my hand. "Good luck," he says, and I march into the station without looking back. No sleep at all, I have to run at three.

Hands Off

I run and win by a long, long way. Set a meet record. But when I finish the bones in my feet feel so hot I can't put them down, especially the left. I limp. Jeanie gets a dark look on her face and says I'm in to the trainer tomorrow, first thing. I limp and limp, and the burning doesn't go away. Jeanie and I have dinner that night. She looks at me closely, like Conner is still written on my face. And he is, *he will always be written on my face*. There are bruises all over my arms, like a kiss. Still warm. So I tell her, a little, and then I tell her about Coach Luke for the first time. She shakes her head down, really hard, like a horse that will not take its bit. "I knew it!" she says, her words fierce. "I knew that was what was happening with you."

She tells me how a couple of months ago he'd tried for her. Taken her to dinner and then come onto her, hard. Given her the same hard luck story about his father. But she'd known better. She'd walked away. And then she started hearing. Whispers about me. Other girls. He had started to give her a hard time in faculty meetings after she turned him down. And the old boys' club on the faculty all followed his lead, the other football coaches, the sprinters. "Damn it," she says, "we're going to get him. You're going to be a champion like this school's never seen. All hands off you." And I knew she was right. I could count on it.

So from then on we have this unspoken pact. Us against them. Each of my victories is a solid mark, a triumph dismembering him, erasing his power piece by piece. Conner, too, who is part of him but is part of me, too *and how I long for those nights like the fire of drink, how badly I am wanting these bruises. He thinks he can bruise me but the marks are mine, twisting him to bits from this place farther than the coldest stars, my meat-locker soul, just tear in. Give it to me, give it to me now and we'll see what you get. I want to break through your teeth, to smash down your wall and to swallow. Glinting eyes, cold mouth. Let me bite you. Like it? Let me bite you some more till you're all marked up. Strip you of your skin. You think you'll have anything left? You've picked the wrong tiger this time. Did you really ever think you were safe?*

So every single 200 in every last practice is a step. Piece by piece by piece; my legs erasing Coach Luke's face. But the burning in my feet is a stress fracture; I have to lay off for six weeks. Off my feet. In a cast. The most important practice time of the season. Everybody says I'll choke again, washed up. I don't know how to bike or swim to stay in shape. I learn.

Jeanie paces the side of the pool, her stop watch in hand, "Come on, Leslie, let's go, you have to do this." Eyebrows raised, shivering in my suit, I look doubtful. It's February cold, maybe forty, and the pool is outdoors, steam rising off it like a Florida swamp. The mountains around us are dead gray. Jeanie's got on Sub-4 sweats and heavy gloves; stripped to the skin I tremble at the thought of even touching the water. I can't swim. My legs are so dense they just sink, and I have to kick really hard just to keep them on the surface. If I let myself hang in the water, within a minute I'll be flat on the bottom of the pool. The last time I swam was maybe seventh grade. Brian, who's a swimmer, has tried to explain what to do, how and when I should turn my head to breathe to match my arm strokes. But when I brace myself, diving in, the water whooshing the breath out of me like a deflated balloon, all I can do is snort like a horse and then choke. It's hard even to get prone. The water's not really so cold, but it stinks of chlorine and feels gritty. My goggles dig into the side of my head, leave suction marks around my eyes like a squid's. My arms flail, choppy, like lawnmower blades, fighting the water, not using it. I'm supposed to swim a hundred, four lengths. My flip turn's pretty weak. Choke snort choke. I make it two and a half and come up coughing. The swimmers, who will churn through this water so smoothly next hour, are already poolside and clowning and rolling their eyes, "Look at the runner." Jeanie's laughing but urging me on. Explaining how swimming will open my lungs, keep them just as tough as our quarters. And I'll be lifting for my legs. So I keep fighting the water, fighting hard.

We get through two hundreds like this. On the third, I'm breathing like an aging truck, and my lungs are filled with white fire. My body is bending and twisting and I'm chopping at the water even worse, the same way I chop at wood. Bending and sinking, seeming to move back just as much as I move up, I am choking when suddenly something straightens out.

I stop fighting and my arms start to smooth over the water like a pond skater-bug, my weight and tightness dropping away. I make it through two laps without choking, and when I get to the side, hanging my arms over the gutter, Jeanie clicks that goddamn stopwatch that seems glued to her hand and says, "Great! You're going to make it, Leslie, you really are," and I believe her. Off my feet for six weeks, weighed down by a cast (both to help the fracture heal and to keep me from running), I'm going to hit this pool like I hit the hills, churning and churning then breaking free, out, flying until my body is left somewhere stopped in its tracks and I continue on without it.

The pool for an hour, then two hours in the training room on the stationary bike, a bike that has one speed, just go. I hate that bike even more than I hate swimming. But I am there in that training room day after day, AC/DC on headphones. How many times can I listen to "You Shook Me"? Quite a few. The notes ring out. They pound and pound like I'm pounding, the floor puddling up my sweat, resistance on the bike so tight it makes my knees weak. I pump for the benefit of everyone who happens to come in, see how hard I am churning this rough wheel around and can understand what that means.

Then off to the weight room, dark, weights clanging, black floor mats, concrete. Me and the football players. No Martha, no girls. The football coach, Vern Friedli, tips his head when I come in. He's coached a few state championship teams, most recently in 1979. The school lives for football and for Vern, so we've got a nice weight room, really nice. Not many girls come here; he watches me, from knee extensions to squats and lunges to a decent bench press, taking very little rest. I do a really nice power clean and he looks at me with something like respect. I always thank him, tip my head back at him when I go out.

In the morning, I get up at five and, trying to move through the house with no noise, go out to the patio, where the exercise bike my father has rented me sits like a relic from a more barbaric time. The moon still out, the cactus eating shadows like leaves. Everything dead quiet till the first flick of my knee sets the pedals in motion like a coffee grinder going round. Even next week seems forever away and all I can do is feel but I try to grind it up in this wheel, torturing the morning with its rasping. Five forty-five Brian shows up to drive me to the pool, where I'll go through my own fumblings in the far-most lane, safely out of the swimmers' way. They are getting used to my flailing, give me tips. I'm still not very fast, but I don't choke. And I feel very lean and hungry. These months, I eat nothing but spinach and shredded wheat. Vitamins. So I'll be sure not to gain any weight.

This spring, when I walk down the halls I feel suspicions all around me. Beth and I still share a locker, but we don't speak. She gives me these looks when Conner comes to talk to me between classes. Her eyes say, "You are fucked up what are you doing," and I know this is what everyone thinks. So many suspicions but jealousy too, even if Conner and I are sparring, because for him to stand there with me in the middle of senior hall is like letting me win one of the earlier rounds, a weakness that may indicate the overall outcome of the fight. Even more, his standing there is a humiliation to Brian, with whom I have not yet broken up. Brian looks over at us quickly, then disappears through the door frame. His friends shield him by giving me looks. He runs with the smart, sarcastic crowd and I can just imagine what they are saying. I get a little red, but Conner's looking at me with that twist to his lip and I would do anything to be standing like this in this public spot with him. The ruling girls in senior hall gather in a cluster and mutter. The guys exchange knowing looks.

Conner and I don't care about any of this. We're involved in something else, something far outside these lockers, these faces, these halls. We feel bold. We look at each other like Frazier and Ali, worthy opponents. He's got this in his voice when he says, "See you later." Cold, but so focused it warms me. My heart leaping up.

Prickly Pear

I miss the first two meets of the season. The rumble is growing: when it comes down to it, Leslie chokes. Spectacular in practice, in dual meets. But when it comes to the big time she chokes, something in her not up to it, some weakness, some crack, a fault line in her fortress we cannot see. Pitching off the cliffs last year, choking in cross-country state, now this stress fracture . . . she'll never recover in time. The very end of March will be six weeks. The cast comes off, and I will run for the first time in a meet, a triple with Sahuaro and Sunnyside. At home, on this track that I owned so well last summer, puking all over its sides. Where I first stepped from the shadows two years ago, pulling ahead to the crowd's delighted screams. I know what people are saying, and Jeanie does too; we both wait.

I tie my green and white ribbons tight. Bend the tops of my fingers down to check my nails, which I keep long that year and in colors like iridescent purple and blood red. Our nails are a major issue on the relays. A few of us wrap them with masking tape to try to keep them from breaking if they're hit the wrong way with the baton. My nails are wine dusk today and perfectly shaped.

I hang with one woman on my team this season, younger than me and twice as crazy. Sandy is a big girl, five-foot ten or eleven, throws the shot-put and discus. Though she's fifteen and doesn't have her license yet, she's been teaching me to drive her old yellow Datsun with the crashed-in end. We walk from the locker room to the bleachers. I'm not limping. My feet feel OK. She's bantering like always, ribbing me like she does when she's teaching me to drive and I go into reverse by mistake, but I can't laugh and can't joke, not this time.

While everyone is warming up and stretching out I find Ray. I'm still in my sweats, my father's old football jersey sweatshirt that I wear each time for luck hanging down below my waist. I've got the sleeves rolled up almost to the elbow, and my hands hang out, every vein and bone. Ray's not changed yet, either. A V-necked Adidas over a long-sleeved T-shirt, Aasics flats on his feet. He's got bony hands, too, bare from the elbow down. I'm still in my flip-flops and he teases me that maybe I should do the mile relay in them just to be sure to protect my feet. The grass on the field is not quite green yet, the hay bales the football players practice off-season blocking on still in place. I push at the track's gray surface with the edge of my foot. The track gives a little. "Well," I tell Ray, "we'll see what I can come up with this time." "Leslie," he says, "you'll be so far ahead it will be *das* after *das,* they won't even be able to even see you." "Thanks," I say, hugging him.

After a while, the sprinter posse arrives, Conner in the lead.

He looks over at me when they come to a stop at the head of the homestretch and gives me a nod, a kind of less-visible equivalent of a thumbs-up. My face gets warm and I smile, looking quickly over to the stands where Brian is to make sure he didn't notice. It's all right, he's talking. I go find Sandy again and we change into uniform. We've got new Dolphin shorts this year, light green, and AMPHI in simple blocks and stripes across the tops. I'm running this meet without spikes, which would put much more pressure on my feet. I'm wearing flats, some blue and white Etonics this time, nowhere near as light as spikes. Because I'm anchoring the 1,600 meter relay, the last event, I worry about this: can I get enough traction? Go up on my toes enough? Our weak link on the relay is the third leg, the girl right before me. The first two runners are strong—Bonnie, our best sprinter, and Michelle, who really *does* look like my sister—but the third leg, Della, is sure to lose some ground, meaning that I'll have plenty to make up. I know my sprinting lungs are strong from hours of burning bikes and flip turns in the pool, where I've finally stopped choking, my legs strong from the sets and sets of knee extensions, but I don't know if I've still got that edge that comes from attacking the curves with quarters exactly on time. I pull the nylon green warm-up jacket over my head, and Sandy squeezes my hand. The 1,600-meter run, slightly longer than a mile, is my first race.

There's a buzz, then a kind of hush when the announcer calls the event and runs down the competitors' names. It's a clear, clear day, but I hear my name as from a distance. Jeanie's right next to the starting line, telling me, 'OK, Leslie, take it out strong, and build it as you go, dropping a second every quarter.' I'm nodding and listening with half an ear, the other half trained on the muttering crowd, my legs tightening and aching for the start. Before the gun goes off I look up quickly, trying to find Coach Luke. Just so I can be sure to blow by wherever he is with a special blend of speed. He's pacing by the head of the homestretch, talking to sprinters, not looking toward me at all. I mark the spot. Coach Estes has put Martha in the 3,200 instead of the 1,600, so I won't be running against her this week. Jeanie's waiting until next week to launch my quadruple: the 1,600, the 800, the 3,200, and the anchor on the mile relay. I'm not going to do the 3,200 today. I look down at my legs for just an instant and notice I'm still pretty white. The end of March and no tan. I hope they look OK, not soft.

The gun goes off and so do I. There are six other girls who are running this race, but I move out quickly and open a space. There's a loud surge of voices, cheers, then I'm into the backstretch where no spectators are. Except that Jim runs up from the other side to cheer me on, then Ray. Jeanie's voice carries over to me: forty seconds, right on pace. I'm on my third hundred, rounding the curve, heading into the homestretch where Coach Luke is, passing the old weight room with AMPHI PANTHERS written over the top in huge white letters. I don't look up, the rising tide of voices carrying me. I head into the last hundred with a burning in my lungs and thighs but nothing in my foot. I feel a little heavy, like a sand-bag truck: this is the very first time I have run in six weeks to the day. I imagine

Coach Luke's eyes on me and draw up, stretching out to the voices lifting me.

I can't hear anyone's feet behind me. Where the finish line will be Jeanie yells my first split: seventy-six seconds for the quarter, right on pace.

By my third lap I'm loosened up, and feel myself growing bigger stride by stride. A spreading warmth all in my chest: I'll show them, they'll see. The voices have all become blurred. On the fourth lap I feel like I'm speeding fast, and when I cross the finish line, there is no one else in the homestretch or even rounding the corner yet. I am dog-beat tired, all tight across my shoulders, but the next runner doesn't come in for half a minute, and the announcer yells out that I have broken my old record and run the state's best time. Jeanie's talking splits with me when I finish, and it's minutes before everyone runs in.

The newspaper barrage begins again—I'm not choking, at least not for the moment. Coach Luke doesn't talk to me but seems uneasy; Jeanie stays close beside me, often seeming to keep her body between his and mine. The next week, the advent of my first quadruple, gets me two headlines: WIND DIDN'T BOTHER HEYWOOD *High winds held down most efforts in high school track yesterday, but nothing could stop Amphi's Leslie Heywood, who recorded the state's top times in two events.* HEYWOOD LEADS AMPHI TO VICTORY *Leslie Heywood won three events.* The press doesn't notice that I actually won four, since our mile relay also wins. That they don't notice, and I do not get any press for this, will influence a decision I will have to make later in the season.

Headlines, paragraphs, I run across pages every Friday—
BUENA HIGH GIRLS REPEAT AS TRACK CHAMPIONS *Buena's triumph, however, could not overshadow the performances by
Amphi's Leslie Heywood*—so much that after a few weeks a
complaint comes in: OTHERS OUTSTANDING *To the Sports
Editor: In consideration that Leslie Heywood is an outstanding runner, there are other outstanding runners in this city. . . .
If compared, Heywood and Atkinson both won three events
last Thursday . . . both led their teams to victories and each
had very amazing times . . . in your article I found Stacy's
name missing against Leslie's for winning three events for her
team. I know other athletes run, throw and jump very well . . .
and they should get some credit. I also feel the public wants to
know about other athletes and their performances.*

I've got other performances too. Conner and I stay on each
other like angry swans. Fierce and sweet. His father buys him
a Jeep; the night he gets it he brings it to show me before he
shows anyone else. We tear off-road, smack into the desert
center, build a fire in a ring of stones and sand. Light glinting
on the spines on the cactus behind, our bodies tearing each
other like spines, we are at each other until we are spent. One
night, we see *Body Heat* at the movies, William Hurt and
Kathleen Turner, and one scene in the bathtub makes us both
shift in our seats, squeeze our hands together tight enough to
leave prints. Turner's character wins in the end, and I can't sti-
fle an excited, "That was great!" when we get up to leave.
Conner agrees with me and I am a little surprised because
Mattie played Ned for everything he was worth and got away

with it. She went for all his weaknesses, strung him along in a carefully planned assault, carried out piece by relentless piece. He ends up in prison. She ends up on the beach. But the tone in Conner's voice has nothing guarded in it.

Driving back, Conner's quieter than ever, singing to himself when AC/DC comes on. He doesn't look at me. At the turnoff to our high school track, he swings the Jeep hard to the right, drives up to the back of the weight room. I look at him. He doesn't say anything. We get out. I watch the tight lines of his jeans disappear over the fence beneath the stadium, into the enclosure where the high-jump pits are kept. He fumbles in his pockets; he's got a key. My ears are ringing a little bit. I jump over myself, tearing my fingers on the metal. Inside, beneath the concrete and boards where the home crowd sits, it's pitch dark and close, and I can smell him, wet sand and mesquite leaves, steam off a blacktop whose core has not cooled after a late monsoon rain. His hands close around my wrists and he pulls me hard. I land on the pits, a slight bounce in the dark; I can't see him. Arms press my arms behind my head. The muscles all along my torso, flat plates of stomach stretch tight, the plateaus of my chest disfigured slightly by the roundness of breasts. Like him, I am almost a perfect line, with little more than muscle and some gristle attaching it to the bone. His mouth is on mine like metal, but I feel like I've got gold teeth. Hipbones grinding. He puts the meat of his thumb against my teeth and tongue, and I hold his face for a moment, my thumbs on his cheeks, my fingers pressed against his temples. Then my arms down tight around him, nails across shoulders, the spread of his traps, hard and smooth and glazed with sweat, a prickly pear torn open. In practice Monday when he takes off his shirt, I see the sprinters look at each other without saying a word, and the quiet smile that flits briefly across Conner's face before he yells out in his best commando voice, "Warm up, warm up, let's go!" and the sprinters and hurdlers all fall in place.

Athletes of the Year

On May 4, I run a 4:52 1,600, which is the fifth fastest in the country, "for a schoolgirl," the paper says, for a *schoolgirl*. "Schoolgirl?" Where do they get this word? It takes away but I have still done it—Coach Luke hasn't looked in my direction for several weeks. Divisionals are at home this year, here on our field for the first time the home crowd can remember. With the state's best times, I'm slated to run my usual triple, along with the relay at the end, which is legal for divisionals but not for state. For state I'll have to give up one event: an athlete can run only three.

Instead of the usual forty to fifty people who show up for the dual meets, the football stadium is packed tonight. Teams in reds and greens and blues, mothers, coaches, fathers, friends. I'm not nervous at all, and Jeanie and I are running down very specific splits to try to knock another second off my 1,600. She's very precise and every meet keeps perfect pace with me back and forth across the track so she's sure to get me my split for each 200. My parents are in the stands tonight, as well as all the other parents who have watched me for three years now, some of whom were beside me a year ago at my hospital bed. But this year, *Leslie Heywood is healthy,* the paper has proclaimed today, *and that means trouble for her rivals.* Trouble indeed. I close my eyes and breathe in deep as I swing my legs to stretch. Conner walks by with Matt Dobbins, headed for the long-jump pits.

Without even thinking I smile at him, wide. (At earlier meets, I've sent Sandy after him with her camera. Sandy's the only one who knows how I feel about Conner, the only one I've told. I get all girly and in between our events we sneak around, following him and hoping he won't see. I giggle and put my hands on her shoulders and point her in his direction, saying look, "You cannot tell me he is not just too hot—you should see how his shirt feels somewhere down along his spine. . . . She rolls her eyes but trudges after him with her camera, gets me several good shots. One of him running a relay. Another holding up a bloody bandage on the bus, when he knows she's shooting him. He and Matt walking, spikes in hands. Him stretching, head down, and the angle of his back showing that his hamstrings are tight. And a beautiful shot of his long jump, airborne. Sandy's a *very good* friend.) He nods. I wonder if he will drive me home from the meet, if it will take us a while to get there. My face gets a little red and I hide it in my stretch and breathe deep in, trying to clear my mind and think the splits. Seventy-twos and 73s for my quarters. And then the announcer is talking about me on the P.A.

I look for Coach Luke again, as I always do before the gun

goes off, then turn away as if I have not noticed. He is look-ing at me this time, steady, flat. Waiting. I look back at him, level, shoulders up, head back, and square off for the start. And when the gun goes off I am so smooth, each stride its own sweet story. I hit each 200 exactly on, split after split. The crowd is with me, rising up through all four laps, and people I don't even know run along the sides to encourage me. I can see only the path in front of me, wide, wide open, clear. I hit the 1,500 mark at 4:33, that magic spot at the head of the stretch where the sprinters always rest, their space. But tonight that spot belongs to me: this time is more than six seconds faster than the state record. I've got a hundred meters left and I open my lungs up like a horse, just like old MJ used to do and I fly, I just goddamn fly, Jeanie's voice carrying me. And I do it. I run faster by a second, hitting the tape at 4:51. The other girls, including Martha, like a stone back in fourth place, come in more than a half-minute later. One down, three to go.

I take the 800 meters in just the same way, the next person a full six seconds behind, and this time the whole crowd is on its feet. Pumped up for me and for the boys' team, who are taking everything, too. By the time I hit the 3,200, the stadi-um is mine. For all eight laps I'm just toking, the air my buoy-ancy, fuel.

There's one quiet spot where no one goes to cheer, the third 200 of the lap, the second curve that runs back along the old weight room. Right at the end of that curve, just before the start of the last 100, Vern Friedli, the football coach, is check-ing tickets as people wander in and out through the fence that separates the football field from the stands. I'm on maybe my seventh lap, and there is not a body near me. The pack is back at the first 100; I'm three hundred yards ahead. I'm locked on cruise, concentrating but noticing some of what I pass.

I've noticed Vern on the first couple of laps, watching. Then he starts to walk around, to pace. Getting ready to go into the final lap and my kick, I happen to look right at him. He's watching me with a smile on his face, just smiling and shaking his head. Our eyes meet, and he looks straight at me, nods his head. And I throw myself into that last lap with what for the world of Amphi is the blessing of the gods upon me. I am an athlete, and Vern Friedli has seen. I am not just a girl tonight, not just a girl at all.

Me and my mile relay team are the only girls who qualify for state. I can run only three events. Jeanie and the other girls, their faces defensive, kind of tight, put it up to me that night: I have to choose. Give up one of my individual events or the relay. I don't need to think about it. I shake my head. I have a much better chance of winning all the individuals, I argue, than our relay has of placing. They look at me like they'd known all along I'd be like this. They knew this is what I would say. I'll head to the state meet alone.

Just before state, Conner talks to me more often and is more tense. We are voted Athletes of the Year, and one day we get to miss class for a photo shoot. Conner stays at my locker even after the bell rings and few bodies are left in the halls. We're in the shade, a cold breeze fingering the edges of my skin. He's standing close, but there's a too-wide space between us that I want to break, my mouth open in my own mind, straight out like a baby bird. I keep it closed. He's looking at me more tender than he ever does, like any second now he would reach across the inches and rest his hand so very gently on my face. "What should we do," Conner says to me. "How should we stand in the picture . . ." his voice trailing off, and in the question opened by the trailing, I know he means, do we stand with our arms around each other or apart. My voice gets really husky and I do my best sarcastic laugh, look up at him with my very best *I'm all yours* eyes, "why don't we shoot some of both?" "Yeah, we will, OK," and he does reach out and take my hand, which feels so warm, so safe, inside his.

His body is so beautiful and straight. The top of my head comes to the hollow of his throat, his shoulders are wider than his hips. Today he's got on his slim-fit 501s and a UCLA Bruins jersey in yellow and blue. We do shoot some photos with our arms around each other, but that is not the one they use. They choose the awkwardness: we're standing outside in the sun, and my hair shines white; we have absolutely no idea what to do with our hands. We're standing maybe two inches apart, my shoulder just above his elbow, his hands two inches up from my hands. He's got his arms bent at the elbow and his palms in front of his navel, pressed together, when they should have been around me. I've got my left hand hiked up a little above my right, and my right hand plays loosely with my fingers on the left, a perfect "O" between my thumb and forefinger. Our arms look like empty triangles used to carrying heavy loads. My hips are narrower than my shoulders, too; I look just as much a straight line. Our bodies look efficient, lean and tight. Of the two of us, I look meaner, eyes squinting in the sun and my lips parted, not in a smile exactly but more like a sarcastic twitch. His smile looks easier, his eyes straight on and calm. I can see myself right now, turning and moving through those two inches so marked in between us and burying my head in his chest, feel his hands stroking my hair and shoulders and holding me. But I didn't turn. I held my head up straight.

Pair of Legs

"Heywood not counting her titles yet." *It's showdown time for Leslie Heywood. Last year, Heywood was one of the favorites to win the distance races at the girls' Class AAA state track and field meet. But two weeks before the meet, she fell off a cliff in the Santa Catalina Mountains, missed divisionals and state. Last fall, she was favored to win the state girls' cross-country individual title. Three days before the race, she caught the flu and had a 103-degree temperature. She completed the race but finished fifth. It is state track meet time again. . . . "Leslie is the best," said Tim Barton, Amphi girls' track coach, "and there's no doubt about it. I think she could be one of the nation's premier milers when she hits her peak. She is definitely an Olympic-caliber runner." Those are strong statements about a girl who until two weeks ago wasn't being actively recruited by a major college. Now she is being courted by Arizona, Arizona State, and Oregon. "This is my last try, my last shot at a state title," she said. "I think I want it more than most."*

I bring the team trophy home from the state meet. I get to keep it for a couple of days before I have to give it back to the school, although since it is my trophy I'm pissed. Second place for the team, just my points, just me. I was the only one who had qualified. I like this. For the past two weeks, I have thought about it all the time, with that rising feeling in my chest like a sweet black smoke. I call it up again—I was the only one who had qualified for the state meet on my whole damn worthless girl-infested team. Thinking this counteracts the sinking, a nagging failure that plays itself across my eyes and through my throat, which feels tight.

HEYWOOD'S 28 POINTS FALL SHORT OF TITLE FOR AMPHI *The Class AAA state track title can't be won on one pair of legs. Not even if they belong to Leslie Heywood. The Amphi High School standout distance runner won two events and came within 10 meters of winning a third in the state meet. . . . She scored 28 points, but that was all Amphi scored, and the Panthers finished second to Phoenix Maryvale.*

Damn. Second place. Second place for the team isn't the only second place I've gotten tonight. I won my first two events, all right, but I missed it on the third, and that's what I play in my head, over and over and over, in the bus seat by myself down the dark highway on the way home, an empty seat in front of me and an empty seat behind, as I wonder about Conner. Too much scraped cactus, too many Friday nights. I wonder if he'll drive me home from the parking lot after the bus but I know he won't because of what I did tonight, which feels good, my face against the glass, which is cold on my cheek. But the excitement in my stomach has a lightness to it that is almost empty.

It had to be him or me, and I was going to get there first. I know girls are supposed to fall in love. Oh, and I love him, but Coach Luke's taught me other things, a coldness even Conner can't erase. I know it's what both he and Coach Luke intended: if they can't break my body, they'll go for the heart. *She thinks she's so great. She thinks she means something. Fine. We'll see. Let's just see if she can take this.* Scanning for signs in the set of Conner's lip, his palms against my face when he touches me, I sensed something had gone slightly wrong in their plan—my face? my eyes? my steady bite? The ways I am like him, the way my body is hard like his, the ways I don't get soft and love?—and Conner felt more than either of them meant him to. Something has come between them, fine as a crack, and he's pulled a little bit away from Coach Luke. I've watched Conner stand close when he talks to him, and square his shoulders a whole different way so they're exactly the same height. Coach Luke's voice was getting tight, and sometimes Conner looked away when he was speaking. This was my advantage, the only chance I'd have.

I did it in the parking lot before we boarded the bus for the state meet, drawn back to my coldest, coldest locked-up place, where not even an echo can reach. I could feel my heartbeat in my neck, the full heat and embarrassment of center stage. This is for all of them: the sprinters, Coach Luke, who walked on the track like they owned it, like I was a trespasser on their turf. For calling me *whore*, *bitch* when I kept on running there, racking up faster and faster times, when I refused to just smile at them as if their acting like they owned the track was OK. For Coach Luke going after me, then Conner, trying to turn me into just some girl with their sex and love and ready sweat. No way. I snarled so fiercely he actually shrank. My sharp, sarcastic best, my sculptured words, not a trace of love or softness in me. "What did you think?" I asked him, the lips that had been all over him now curling back from my teeth. I was speaking from some far-off place where everything was liquid, hot. He'd never seen anything, I imagined, quite like this. "Just what was it you thought I was doing? Did you think for even a second I had feelings for you? Oh, I've had a feeling, and its name is hate. I have hated you this whole damn time. You make me sick. I never want to speak to you again." He didn't say anything and took a few steps back, getting a little white. Once he said my name. And I laughed at him. I laughed and turned my back, each stride away from him a shot from an MX-10.

Conner was the captain of Coach Luke's team and they were used to his pumping them up. But on the bus to Phoenix he sat by himself. He did not say a word. And on the track when he warmed up his strides looked off, like something wasn't right. The other guys got knocked off stride. Used to his voice keeping them in line, they dropped a baton on the relay. Someone else tripped over a hurdle. Everyone was off on the sprints. Conner was smaller. His long jump faltered. He couldn't extend. And I laughed. I was terrible. Terrible. Enormous. Big. I was *Body Heat*. My name over and over from the P.A., I was the meet.

But damn it! there's this other thing, this flaw in the whole damn machine. It was the two mile: I led the whole race, with only one runner near me. Heading into the final lap she dropped back, and I thought everything was safe and I just needed to kick in, my legs and lungs so regular I couldn't feel the ground or the wind. But three hundred yards from the end something gave and I started to feel it, wet and warm down my leg. I forgot the other runners and forgot the track and all I thought was, can they see it, can those faces yelling and cheering my name in the crowd see my shorts getting wet, darkened by something that isn't sweat? I pulled my stomach in tight to try to stop it and my stride shut down but I didn't think there was another runner near me. I couldn't hear a sound. Pulling my stomach in didn't work. It just ran down my leg like a warm wash of blood but more embarrassing and I tried to get outside myself to see if they could see it and I kept trying to keep it in as I tried to open my stride back up but I could feel it making its way, languid, soft to my shoes and I brought my legs closer together and it was *there,* there, in that last ten yards, there was someone else and she went by me like cotton, like leaves blown to the side flying under car tires and by the time this dawned on me it was over.

Now I look outside the window at the glancing light, the gentleness of early summer, and damn, damn, if that just hadn't happened it would have been the perfect night. But it did. I am not large enough not quite larger than life not quite yet a machine can't contain my own pee like some cosmic god laughing at me shoving all my weakness in my face. If I just hadn't cared, then all of the people who thought that I lost because I was tired, because I was not tough enough to win all three, would know they were wrong, would know that it was only that I let myself be a girl that made me fuck up like that and let her by me. Two strides. If I had stretched for two strides I would have still been ahead and 28 points is pretty good but I want all 30 and damn it now, God damn it, damn, and this is all I can think about, how I fucked up, so when people congratulate me my voice is hollow and flat with an edge. The only thing that lifts me is what happened to the guy's team, Coach Luke, who had to congratulate me, who had to look at me in the parking lot with that second-place trophy, when they all choked so bad they got nothing, my points alone were *more than all of theirs put together and they have to acknowledge it, admit defeat because it's been a war and I have won.* Even though I fucked up the last race, they still have to bow and acknowledge my place and Coach Luke is so pissed they leave early, before any of the scores are called and I see them get into their bus and leave and I laugh, the perfect revenge, I couldn't have done it any better but still, something feels hollow, not just quite right.

Biggest Ego

The next morning is worse than not quite right. It's May; light's early, I'm up and ready to run. Like always, I wake thinking this, but something is not the same. I open my eyes in my narrow bed and it's so palpable I almost say, "What?" to the silence and sit up to check. The room *looks* the same. The shag of orange carpet is still underneath my feet. My dresser is still against the opposite wall, its corners nicked, exposing the pressure board inside. The wall-length mirror, loaned to me by my mother, is still hanging over my bed, and it gives my face back to me a little white. Are the walls the same distance from each other as they were when I fell asleep? I don't know if the room feels more open or more close, or maybe it's both. I know the light has its usual May fierceness, for I can already feel the heat coming in right behind it.

Vete a la chingada. Where was I? Sound of cicadas and mourning doves, check. Clothes in my closet, check. So, what? What is it? My stomach is strangely hollow, that carpet is *not* caressing my feet. I sit at the edge of the bed with my hands locked down tight either side of my legs; I've never felt anything quite like this. Was my father yelling at my mother as I slept? My mother yelling something at me? I listen. Silence. School, and I've forgotten some key test? No, the meet was on Saturday, so this would be Sunday. No school. What else? Brian? No, we split when I went to the prom with Conner. Conner? Nope. Threw away that one. Coach Luke? Chastened for the moment. Well, then *what?*

It comes like a whisper: *the state meet is over.* Over. Done. You won. *So what next?* Maybe a short run, a three-miler. Fall's a ways away, not much need to train now. And oh, yeah, there's the paper. See if they say, HEYWOOD ALMOST WINS ALL THREE. Almost. Two, anyway, better than none, ink for the record books: HEYWOOD'S 28 POINTS FALLS SHORT OF TITLE FOR AMPHI, they say. And, yes, there is something, that makes my pulse pick up, my heart race, warmness all over my chest. Something, quite something, yes. Because of me the articles from *both* papers focus only on the girls' meet. In a reverse of what always happens in the articles about big meets, this time only two short paragraphs go to the boys. Because of me. Today, for this moment, in this really small way, I have overturned the world. For the moment, *but what next?*

My parents don't say much. I go for a short run and then try to find something to read. My mind can't stay on the words. I sit on my bed, staring at the oleander branch against the window and thinking the leaves look sharp. I get up and pace. Who can I call? Since I had turned on Conner and Brian wasn't speaking to me, that left out a phone call or a date. I'd spent most of my free time with Conner the past three months. It's Sunday, so if I want to call Jim I'll have to wait until his family gets home from church. I don't know what we could do anyway.

I won, but there is nothing to celebrate in this quiet that hangs all around me like lead. I think about the next day, when they will announce over the school P.A. that I am the state champion. I guess I should be still and not smile when I hear it and shrug whether people congratulate me with that tight tone in their voice or if they really mean it when they do it. It doesn't matter; *emptiness still. A champion of emptiness, a champion without a spine or blood, just some airy whistling, maybe. Like wind through pines I haven't seen since those summer forests, my sorely missed green, some indefinable bloom I can't find. The emptiness is all over me, clamping tight: the meet is won, and I literally do not know what to do. Where to stand, to rest. Where to put my hands. What now? And what next?*

Graduation is the next weekend. My parents decide not to come: it's just high school, they figure, they'll have many other graduations to attend, and an advanced degree means more. It feels like I'm the only one with no one in the stands. Beth's mother gives me a hug. Brian's mother gives me a sideways look. I sit down on the field, with everyone around me kind of buzzing. I smile and wave when I see Jim and Victor and Ray and start to get up, but they're all talking to their parents. So I just sit. There's this big party after, held on a property the Wexlers own on the other side of Sabino Canyon, in the middle of the dry river bed hung low with scrub brush and mesquite. I go with Sandy, who is the only one who runs up to me when the ceremony's finished and we're all dismissed. There are bodies everywhere. Everyone is milling around, laughing, talking, in groups that keep shifting. Some hearty shouts ring out, contained by the pressure of left-over heat, hanging in the still-warm air feathering itself above the sand.

Sandy and I stand several feet back from the action. She's a sophomore, and I'm the senior with the biggest ego according to the class vote and where that vote was recorded in the year-book. My heart down in my stomach when I read it, glad to make it onto the list, but I don't have words to explain to any-one why this, biggest ego, isn't right.

In a twist that saved it, Conner was voted it, too. Both of us, together, Biggest Ego, Conner Stevens and Leslie Heywood. Well the egos aren't speaking to each other tonight, and I don't even feel like I've got one. Beth was voted Best Dancer and Best Musician. Brian got Most Likely To Succeed. But the biggest ego isn't sure who to talk to, what to say. I feel lonely. Then I don't care; I talk and don't remember to whom or what I say. I lose Sandy at some point. And I'm feeling, where did it all go? How could it all just fly away? What's happened to my life? I keep looking around for Conner. I can feel where he is standing, however far. I keep imagining he will come up from behind and put his hand on my shoulder, and we'll walk out into the sand and pick up just like nothing has happened. He doesn't. If I turn in his direction, he looks or walks away. I stay for a long time, hoping. Long into the night.

I've lost Sandy for good and am wondering how I'll get

home when I see Brian. He pulls back a bit the way you would when you first see a scorpion or maybe a rottweiler. But then he sees the look on my face and moves closer. Starts to talk to me. And as the light turns we spend hours in the Escort again, just talking. I try to convince him to take me back, even though he is going to Stanford in the fall. He doesn't take me back, exactly, but he leaves the door open for hope. He takes me home. He takes me in his arms, and he kisses me goodnight. And I get home and my mother asks me, quite grumpy, where it is I've been all night. *Nowhere, mother, nowhere at all.*

One gray soulless day marches into the next and it seems I've lost Conner for good. What did I expect? But I can't stop thinking about him, not a bit. I drive my father's Toyota pick-up to practice until I can get the Bug my mother's given me for graduation, though I'm supposed to pay her back for it. The Toyota's got good speakers, and I listen to the Alan Parsons Project, *Pyramid,* especially "Eye in the Sky." With the windows down it blasts out good and everyone can hear it. I know that Conner often drives the same route along Skyline Drive, and I always look for the El Camino or the Jeep, hoping I will see him while this song is on and that he will hear it, although why I'm not sure because, unlike the speaker in the song, neither of us seem to have access to each other's minds, only to silence, and there's been an awful lot of that since state. I've signed a letter of intent with Arizona; he's going to Colorado; whatever world we have shared has gone past us. I know this. But it doesn't matter; I still keep thinking I will run into him, and we won't say a thing, just head to the trails off from Valley View Road, pick up where we left off. I am sure of it. So sure.

I do run into him one night, at the stoplight at Skyline and Campbell. I'm heading west and he's heading east. I yell out the window, trying to make my voice casual and not shake, "Conner, hi, I've got the prom pictures, do you want to see them?" His eyes get a little dark, and he turns his head so I'm getting the hatchet of his profile. "No," he just says, and stares straight ahead. "All right," I say, a little smaller, "well, call me sometime before you go away." "OK," he says, and the light has changed. Heading east. Heading west.

I've kept a couple of those pictures, a 5 × 7 and a wallet-size, in a scrapbook with the track shots. Against the sandy background of hotel wallpaper, surrounded by fake-looking tropical plants that were actually alive, I sit in the rattan captain's chair with Conner standing by my side. My right arm rests on the arm of the chair and my forearm's raised up, my hand enclosed within his hand. He's got big hands, and inside his mine looks small—delicate even—only the second and third finger visible between his forefinger and thumb. My thumb's bent in, his rests on top of mine. The edge of his tux falls across the top of my bicep, which, because my forearm is up, stands out nicely. He's very tall, so sitting, my head is just below the level of his chest, where the lapels run together and the ruffles fade. He's standing stock straight, his shoulders high, more than halfway up the wall. He looks at the camera, and his eyes are level, not glinting, even a little kind. But he's still got that crooked smile, the right side of his mouth wider than his left. My eyes are confused and my smile looks pasted on, half way between frightened and goofy. It's not a good hair day, the way it's braided too flat across the top, and the tiny white flowers don't work. I'm much too tan for my white eyelet dress, tan with a reddish cast, a little cooked. With my hair back like that my nose looks too big.

We did not have a good time that night. I saw Brian with whoever he was with—some swimmer from another school—and felt something rise in my chest like a wary dog, who is this girl and what am I doing? Why am I standing here with Conner, why do I do these things? The hotel where maybe eight of us turned in for the night was nothing like the cactus and open sand, and I didn't feel much like sex. I put up some resistance at a certain point and Conner got annoyed. I didn't feel like fighting him or maybe felt partly that I owed him: on the measuring stick of who-is-committed-to-and-controlling-whom, the prom is a public declaration. This must have been the weekend before state, a few days before I turned on him.

Three years later I will write to him in Boulder, Colorado. I don't know how I got his address; I suppose I must have called his parents. Dear Conner, I said, what did I say? I told him with some racing words he was still beating in my blood. That I never lost the feel for his teeth. That the night in my bedroom before that indoor meet was the night I return to again and again when my bones begin to ache, that nothing else ever measures up. I told him to call me when he got back into town, and for two years running, Thanksgiving and Christmas, he did. Called me in the middle of the night without saying his name and I always knew right away who it was. I gave directions without question. We hardly spoke. But it had lost the pitch, the biting of that first night, or the night on the high jump pits when we both lost sections of our skins and what else? The last year he called I was in love with someone else and I ignored it. Let it ring. Let it ring.

The last time I saw him, our tenth high school reunion, I had just gotten a job and a Ph.D. My hair was short; he was married. Our eyes blank we had nothing whatever to say. I tried to act so calm, so detached, and I did. But what I really wanted to do was to shove him down in the back room, reclaim him. Reclaim myself. I didn't. And he looked at me like he'd never seen me, like he had no idea who or what I was. When he left the room, I felt the broken places in my mouth like glass.

Bum Steer

Now I've got something else to take care of. For a long time, my mother has been after me to prosecute Coach Luke. I never told her what happened in the first place, but I talk in my sleep. At least that's what she tells me. My screaming about him in the middle of the night, muttering, hysterical fears about pregnancies and legs. In my sleep, loud enough to wake her up. So she confronts me with it and I have nothing to say. It's not something you can talk about, especially not to someone who judges you.

My mother wants me to turn him in to the school board. *He's evil,* she says. I say no. Last year, when she first started in, I begged and pleaded, asked her to remember how fast I was running with him. How important it was that I ran fast senior year. Told her how hard it would be for me in school if I did this, how people would look at me like I was diseased. There would be more construction barricades and dead mice, more songs about Leslie the whore. I cried. I yelled. I said, a year.

Just wait until I graduate and I'll do it then. She backed off, but she didn't like it. I hoped she'd forget but she hasn't.

Now I've graduated, and she starts the old litanies again. But turning him in is the last thing—partly—that I want to do. I'm still afraid of people's stories, the names they would call me, what they would say. The way I would walk around and everyone would look at me with hating eyes. I'd be marked like there was something wrong with me, some flaw that makes me not fit in. No, no, I say but she insists. She won't leave me alone with it.

I'm sitting at the kitchen counter where I sat with Coach Luke that night a year ago, and she is talking fast, looking straight at me like she's going to move me no matter what. That same kind of wanting-me-to-do-something in her voice.

"He's a predator," she says. "I've heard there have been other complaints. He can't keep doing this to you and keep getting it swept under the rug. It isn't right. You have to stand up for yourself. You're strong."

I shake my head. That's a good one. Since when does she want me to be strong? She's always tried to beat it out of me, make me a girl like she thinks girls should be. Quiet. Obedient. Good. The opposite of me. Girls who are quiet and good are victims. I'm not a victim of anything.

I close my eyes and breathe out a long breath. I'm tired. I don't feel particularly strong. "I'd rather not turn him in," I tell her.

"You have to," she says. "It's the only way you can redeem this. It's your responsibility, the only way you can make sure he won't do it to other girls." *The only thing that will keep you from being a whore.* She doesn't actually use those words, but this is what I hear her say, and part of me believes her.

I have terrible feelings about this, reasons I don't want to do it. Part of me agrees with her: *what he did was wrong and he should pay for it.* But not in the way that she thinks. He should pay for all of it, for the way before anything happened he looked at me like I didn't exist. For what the tone in his voice, the words under his words, made me into: *You're a girl, so you're garbage, not an athlete, no right to be here with my guys on my field.* The way he walked like he owned the place: *We just use girls for sex, and we don't know why you think you're any different. Come here, little girl. Just who do you think you are? We'll show you you're no different.*

Who do you think you are? How many times has my mother said this to me in exactly the same way? But now she is saying that I will be glad I did this, that it will help me respect myself later. She keeps throwing words at me like "predator," "civic duty," "saving other girls." She says it's simple: he's an adult, I'm a child, and he is a monster who has violated me. When I shake my head, she insists so fiercely that I know she will think I'm something awful if I don't agree with her. "It's so obvious," she says. "How could you think anything else?"

But I do think something else. "It wasn't just him," and I think but can't say *there were times when I lit up at the look in his eyes, times I wanted to sit still beside him. How I wanted him to see me, my strides on the track, my towering fierceness just for him. Out of all those girls, I imagined he would say,* out of everyone, you are the one I can't forget. The one I can't just throw away. *How I wanted to be the one he sees, the one who gave him guts and perfect hundreds, my loving arms, my quiet mouth, the preciseness of my splits.*

I did it. I gave. It's not like he held me down with a gun and forced me. Not like he read me my rights. We fought a good fight, and I won it my own way. I don't want to report it, I just want to forget the whole thing. But she won't let me: *Something is wrong with you if you don't do this. You're not my daughter when you act like that. My daughter would be good. If she had sex with anyone, it would be because he forced her. Predator. My daughter would say this, do whatever she could to redeem it. Show she's worth something, not like the screwup I fear she is.*

I have to do what it takes to make her think I'm OK, not family baggage, not the black sheep you'd throw outside. So feeling all twisted over, hot and cold, lighter and darker, I agree to tell the school board about Coach Luke. But I don't know what I feel about any of it. I don't know what is right.

It feels like everything good about my life is finished, and I've got to get through this whole lonely summer, which stretches out like an open mouth. I work as a lifeguard at the same pool as Brian and run sprints with Jeanie on the junior high track, but both of these relationships, if I have to be realistic about it, are over. I try hard not to think about everything: college, having to run on a new team, or, especially, this case against Coach Luke, which my mother has already started.

He gets a lawyer to represent him, the mother of one of my

friends on the guys' cross country team. His testimony is that nothing ever happened. His lawyer goes after the overactive imagination angle, paints me as the oversexed, high-strung girl. Some people know that I love to write. Someone, I don't know who, must have told his lawyer about this, about a novel I've written. Maybe it was him. The lawyer contacts my English teacher, who is reading it. He gives her the pages, some tortured words with a fierce heroine at their center. "You see how she likes to make things up," his lawyer tells the school board, as they sit there riffling through my pages. "You see how she likes to exaggerate things, what a good storyteller she is. She probably misinterpreted one of his looks and imagined the rest. And she does go around with a lot of boys, you know, here is a list of their names. . . ." They contact Beth and Teresa to testify, tell everything they know about me, about Coach Luke, about what happened.

Sometime in July I have to go testify. I get the time off from work and drive in my Bug to the administrative offices off Prince Road, very near where Coach Luke lives in a nest of white adobe condos lying along Limberlost Drive. Near Coach Luke's bedroom, where I went only that once.

My skin's burned red, my hair is white from all of the chlorine and sun. I'm wearing shorts and a T-shirt over my lifeguard suit. The shock of the air conditioning as I walk in is like walking through a bucket full of ice. There are six old men at a table in a close room that is much darker than outside in the sun. One of them asks me to sit down, waving his arm at a chair on the side closest to the door.

They start talking, run through allegations, testimonies, different parties' beliefs. "We need to ask you some questions that may be uncomfortable to answer, please be as direct as you can." I hear these words from far away and I am not sitting in this room because *tell us*, I hear a voice saying under the actual words, *about how he touched you his lips on your skin and his fingers inside you and his tongue along your mouth and how far you threw your head back when he entered you from behind.*

"Sexual intercourse," someone says, "tell us about this," and my mouth is open and I am speaking in a flat tone and my mother is there I know because of the detail she tells me later but I don't see her right now, I don't see anything.

I am speaking some words and these words are coming out of me like stones, dissected frogs that are numbered already, dead, and I am waiting for the scalpel that will descend and cut them up and *remember*, I start talking in my head to Lisa, my friend, *that year in tenth grade, that biology lab when we snuck in after class and set all those croaking frogs free? Them leaving a trail, getting the concrete a little slimy, a little wet?* And another man is saying, "Miss Heywood, how many times?" and just to my left there is a white head bobbing and lots of ties and oxford shirts, "And did you," one of them is saying, "enjoy it? Did you want to do this with your coach?"

I know I am saying something but I have no idea at all what it is because in my mind I am *running down a dark hall and everywhere there are feet sticking out expecting me to trip and I work very carefully to avoid them shifting a little to the right and then left trying to turn my head enough to hear what's coming at me from behind and this is scarier than any quarter because I don't know where the marks are and which one is my lane* and someone says "Miss Heywood," and I bump my head up, "do you have anything else to say?" *and there he is behind me with a stopwatch in his hand and he is pouring whiskey all over me and it is running down my thighs and I can't do a thing to stop it* and they have decided that they have heard enough.

They dismiss me like a bad student from class and I walk out firmly, but I am shaking and colder than I ever was, broken out in goose bumps in July. I can't find the right key to open my car. I keep trying the wrong one, and when I finally get the door open I don't look for any traffic, I just drive.

My mother tells me later I pull directly in front of a speeding truck, which swerves violently to the side; I hear nothing at all and just drive back to the pool and get up in my chair and watch kids swim.

So I testify that it happened and he testifies that it didn't, and words and words later this is where we are. So finally they ask me if I will take a lie detector test. I am no longer reluctant to speak. I can't believe that Coach Luke and his lawyer— my friend's mother—are saying I'm making it up. How can they say that? And I can't believe that anyone would believe them. Regardless of anything I might feel about it, it did happen. I didn't make it up.

I ask them when they want me to take the test, and a date is set for the next week. But before this day comes I get the final word: they have asked Coach Luke to do it, too, and he has decided to resign his job instead. My mother is triumphant. She says it is all settled now, we've made the world safer for other girls, set a precedent, and decency has been restored. And am I more decent, safer from myself? My stomach leaps up like it does right before and after a really important race, my heart inside my ribs like an empty well.

Late that summer, I am out with Teresa one Friday night, dancing at a bar. I think it is called The Bum Steer. I'm feeling a little lonely. It's one of those nights I'm waiting for something—I don't know what—to happen, but it never does. We're drinking, laughing, the music is loud and the buzzing fray of voices is enough to take you out of yourself for some moments. But I'm following Teresa like a puppy who doesn't know the right moves: where to stop exactly, where to pee on the bush, where to run and where to let the cars pass by slowly. I don't remember who we are dancing with, probably Sandy's brother and some of his friends, and negotiating the small path Teresa's body makes, I'm following her across the bar to a table. Suddenly she stops and shoots a look at me over her shoulder, like she's seen a dead body, almost, or someone with a gun. And I look to see what it is she is warning me about and I almost run smack into him. Coach Luke. And first I feel as if I've knocked my head against a low-hanging beam and stagger back, but then I recover myself and we're both laughing.

This is funny. *Of all the places, of all the bars in town . . .* He asks me if I want to dance and I say sure. He takes my hand and leads me out and we keep laughing. *I'm sorry,* I want to say at first. *You gave me a good fight and I won but I did-n't mean it.* I look at his eyes, still with that sarcasm in them but with something else too, something I really need. *Maybe he doesn't hate me.*

Our bodies move toward each other but not too much, sepa-rate but our hands touch. *I'm that irresistible, maybe, a mark no indifference can erase.* Then I notice he's smiling kind of funny.

Why? He had to leave his job because of me, and here he is smiling and holding my hands. *How can he stand here and hold onto my hands when this was a war and I have won it?* I start to breathe shallow, a little faster now in the loud, close heat. The other bodies seem to press toward us as we look at each other and I think *doesn't he get it? Won it. I won the war, damn it.* I won.

There is a love that grows in forgotten places, like a weed, where it is not supposed to grow. There is no one who wants to own it, and it knows. It grows on the face where a fist has hit, craves the shininess of blue, even after the blood has returned to the veins and the arteries where it lives. It grows wherever a body has marked you, imprinting your flesh with its flesh. Denied, this love will eat you up, will eat all other loves. Black crows against a green, green wheat, it takes you in dark spaces, corners you're never supposed to go. Longing the return of a fist at midnight, a dick like a club, that blunt. A love blind in its hunger, no eyes for anything but the blows. It marks souls, souls who in their sadness, love, are broken dogs who return to their owners out of the deepest kinds of faith. The name for this love is sickness, but it is an act of faith.

PART THREE

Never Enough

Cross-country in college is a trip. All that running in a pack, running with girls, really fast girls, who I have to win against every day. I know I have been pushing too hard. I know that even though the landscape is still the same, the quarry rock and the narrow trails turned over by only a very few feet, running with these women, on this team, is not the same. This driving in me, something broken or unsprung like a watch stuck only on go, that can never stop to rest, not ever, until it just winds on down to silence, this driving is winding me too tight. I weathered high school like this, but it is different now, these women with fast and shapely legs who have won just as many races as I have, whose lungs and longings are also in sync.

Still I have managed to hold most of them off, except Kim. Cute, smiling everywhere, loud-mouthed Kim, for whom Arizona is clearly the sticks, so far ahead of the rest of us she is to us just like I was to the other girls at Amphi. So thin, such a tiny little butt and glamorous twisting hair and all the best sweats from her sponsors, which none of the rest of us have, glamorous even if she does have braces on her teeth. The most delicate little muscles in her arms and around her neck a gorgeous gold chain that glows softly, which she sometimes puts in her mouth after a really nice sweat. Beautiful lips. Nails longer almost than her fingers.

She doesn't train with us much, preferring her brother for a coach, and I feel positively pedestrian by her side. I know I cannot beat her even as I fix my hungry eyes on her and try. Just last summer, when I was teaching kids to swim and trying to keep my mind off Coach Luke, Kim was winning major races like the 800 at the National Sports Festival, breaking the record set by Mary Decker Tabb (who later became Mary Decker Slaney, but we all remember her as Mary Decker), the one so far out in front of us that running that fast is not even a dream but for Kim it is more than a dream. She has run the 800 a full *thirteen* seconds faster than me and clearly, so clearly I am out of her league as she manages to let all of us know just as I let everyone know last year as I was stomping around the Amphi stadium insisting on knowing all my splits while everyone else was still finishing their race. Kim laughs and talks to me a few times, just a few, because I am also pretty, though not as pretty as her, and because I have finished consistently second behind her in the cross-country races throughout the season.

Sixteen seconds in front of me in the first meet. I am clearly the number two even though I have a few challengers and I am not as far ahead of them as Kim is ahead of me. Kim and I get the headlines in the campus paper. FRESHMEN REPLACE CROSS-

COUNTRY ALL-AMERICANS (and this is what is so harrowing, how very easily you get replaced, I feel it in my gut every time I see it, like a cold soda gone down way, way too fast). The article makes clear that while nobody thought much of me before, my high school record not that impressive, I am starting to carve myself out a place *(how exhausting it is, all this carving. Some afternoons before practice I sit stretching in my dorm room thinking I have already given so much, all my blood and my driving, pounding heart and guts, I can not possibly keep doing it, giving it more and again. I have been doing it so hard for the last three years and now this is the fourth and it is so much harder and all my old strategies just don't quite work and I know it in me somewhere but all I know how to do is to drive and to drive and to give and to give and never stop and since I don't know what else to do I just try giving more but I am so tired)*: Another freshman, Leslie Heywood, has run somewhat unrecognized by everyone but her coach and opponents. The rest of the article focuses on me and how I will deal with tougher competition in the upcoming invitational.

The meet is in San Diego's Balboa Park, which is filled with ancient palms and replicas of Spanish haciendas, broad green lawns winding through the hush of patches of tropical plants. It's warm, so we get out of the van with little more on than our uniforms, made by Sub-4, which stands for the sub-four-minute mile. None of us except Kim and all the guys have ever come close to this, although all of us girls have gone quite significantly sub-five. Our uniforms are really nice, bright blue with white stripes, our tops just the reverse, white with blue stripes, and Arizona, the logo, with a big red "A" in front of the rest of the letters in black, a green cactus rising up out of the "i" with a jagged line of mountain behind it. I'm happy with how it fits me, for I am really thin right now, my body-fat percentage under the ten percent figure Coach Dougherty says all of ours must be. Really sweet biceps and quite nice shoulders, well-defined, though in the race I'm leaning back a little, too much to get full speed—I should be further forward. And, oh, I am concentrating, my mouth set, my chin up, my ears tuned like a wolf's on the footsteps I am hearing behind me. We are nearing the finish line, and all these people are lined up, watching. My shoulders back and my mouth pursed tight, this grim determination counteracted only by the real softness of my face and that hair curled and pulled back and floating behind my shoulders, not even sweaty, my green and white ribbons traded for blue and white, our colors, with just a little bit of red.

My forehead is clear and my chin is up and my skinny arms just right for a distance runner, but my legs are just too god-damn big. The quadriceps are overdeveloped, too big for my hips. Floating right behind me is Anthea James, a senior, my biggest challenger on the team, breathing smooth, her eyes closed, but I am staving her off, which I do all the way to the finish line though just barely. Anthea's from South Africa, and she's got really thin legs. She's tired, and my mouth is straining, and I am thinking Jeanie always said that *for a distance runner you've got the power of a sprinter, Leslie; Leslie, you simply need to learn to use your strength because there is so much of*

it there if you can feel it and I try to feel it and think it right
now so I can tip myself into a sprint and I do. Anthea's flying
feet don't catch me and I finish the race nice and clean. A great
finish. But I am eighteen, and my face is starting to look old.

Our team pictures are taken at the head of the very trail I
was running on when I fell off the cliff two years before. I
do not mention this to anyone, for I am someone else now
and that confusion is buried: the sprinters no longer exist.
The sprinters on this team are different. There is some professional expectation to running here that make me stand up
taller, that makes the high school sprinters and Coach Luke
seem a hundred years away. In the picture I stand, tan legs
against the desert sand, the cliffs of rock I fell off, my head
reaching over the mountain that looks like it's part of a water-
color painted in from behind. My hand is on my hip and my
smile is pasted on again, but my body is straight. I am still
wearing shoes that are too small for me, size six when I need
size eight. I get blisters all the time. But the way I am standing
doesn't show it.

In the team picture there are fifteen of us, all except Kim, who
was not available for the pictures that day. She rarely ran with
us but when she did, I did my very best to keep up. If she was-
n't there I finished each part of the workout first, no slacking
even for a second. Anthea was always right behind me. In the
picture, she is catercornered from me, part of the back row
that's standing while I'm one of the six who is squatting in front.
This could be an awkward position, but I am posed in a way
that brings my hamstring out just right. The other girls have legs

that are thin-roped and straight, and we are all very thin. I'm smiling too widely again—it really looks fake this time—squinching up my eyes. Nine of the fifteen of us are blonde. One redhead. Five brunettes. We all have grade point averages over 3.5, and personalities that would be categorized as Type A.

Every weekday afternoon the team meets at McHale Center at 2:30 or 3:00, depending on how long Coach Dougherty plans to talk. Sometimes he talks a lot. And then we're into the van, up Oracle Road past my old high school, out to the golf course where we do drills and long runs or a series of shorter timed runs. The workouts are never easy, and I hate the drills and stretching. I'm anxious to get to the real workout and get it over, managing to stave off any other challenge for maybe one more day, thinking *stuck, Leslie, you're really stuck, you run far too much at one speed. Downshift a little, darling, why don't you? But I can't, no I can't I can never give in if I stop for a second, if I stop for a day I might never get started again and then I will be lost, really lost, invisible even, I will not know where to go or what to do with my body in late afternoons and early mornings and no one will even know my name and will certainly not know where to find me or notice I am missing . . .*

We all get personalized workout sheets, handwritten in a scrawl that sometimes seems to dictate our lives. We are broken into groups. My workouts are the hardest, confirming my place at the head of the team; Coach has seen me running my guts out on every rep and understands that this girl, this one, will give as much as anyone can take. A really good coach would have understood that the best thing you could convince this girl to do was stop training so hard and rest, but in the scientific data that most coaches base their workouts on, it wasn't until the '90s that rest was recognized as part of training.

It is still so hot that cicadas are buzzing in the trees, and the sprinklers hiss off and on all around us, bugs gathered in the heaviness left behind. We finish stretching and listen some more to Coach, who has a philosophy about all the reps that we've done, and he wants us to know it and get it exactly straight. The trainers break out the bright orange tubs of Gatorade they mix for us every day, and we gulp it down, our blood feeling a little like it is coming back to life. Most of us switch to water right away to make sure not to take in too many extra calories. Gatorade: 120 calories for six ounces; the plastic cups we're given hold eight. The slower girls don't switch to water, the "B" string girls who aren't on scholarship and don't run in every meet. They're always the first to admit they're tired, to laugh and to joke when we get back in the van, heading for the training room to get weighed and then to the weight room to complete our prescribed sets of reps and sets. They don't even like to lift weights, and often complain about it. I love the weight room more than almost anything. Everyone tells me not to lift so heavy, but I have 100-pound incline bench and a 225 squat. It's the training room, before the weights, I don't like much. We compete there, too. All of us get quiet and shifty, dropping eye contact, looking at each other's stomachs for the faintest shift gathering the front of the shorts, a bulge to indicate an ounce more weight. We hold our stomachs in, keep our steps smaller, heads and shoulders toward the ground. The trainer isn't helping us out much. "Eliza, 112! Ann, 108! Leslie, 110!" he yells as we get off the scale, as if we can't read the numbers ourselves. *Just tell everyone why don't you. Just tell Reggie and Carter sitting right over there looking at my legs and sizing them up. My butt. See that little jiggle right there, this patch of fat right over my knees? Just let them know how much I weigh, how much fat I am carrying over these bones and I will be forever ashamed and I will promise you promise you not to eat, not to put anything inside me that might slow me down like potato chips or ice cream or pizza or vodka at midnight or even frozen yogurt and I will whisk pure I will whisk clean I will put nothing like this in me and I will turn into the clearest flame so pure and I will sprout wings upon these feet and I will fly past you, gone . . .* I'm sure the football players are listening and will snort in laughter if one of us weighs too much. I always cringe as I step up to the scale, so certain it's coming.

Sometimes during the week Coach Dougherty makes us eat dinner with him at his house near the golf course, because his wife is a nutritionist and is going to teach us how to eat. We get handwritten sheets that address this, too. But sitting through a meal with us is a true horror. As we stand in line with our empty plates in the kitchen waiting to get at the serving bowls, steaming hot, the hours of workout burning us up, metabolisms kicked to the very clouds in the sky with nothing whatever to feed them, we are starving, low-blood-sugar fierce. But we are also looking fiercely, each one of us casting our eyes down and to the side to see what goes on everyone else's plate and how much, counting these new calories, will be added to the store of fat on this or that girl's thighs already. Well, for some of us it is thighs. For some of us it is stomachs. I have a problem stomach, only the top two squares ever visible, not the six I should be able to see. My lower stomach, between the hipbones, ugh. We all know without saying it the exact distribution of fat and problem spot on each of us. Veiled glances, strained silence, as we sit down to put that food into our mouths, feeding the emptiness lying in wait. Each mouthful we consume is a downfall, each mouthful we refuse is a victory, a vindication of our purity and the spread of our bones and flying feet that will take over the warm, warm winds. We are perfect, fueled and well-oiled, well-tended machines, taking just enough mouthfuls to keep us primed. I followed Coach Dougherty's instructions to the letter, only sometimes going him one better.

In the little time we're not together, we all do some running by ourselves or in pairs. One day on a long, slow distance run with one of the guys from the men's team I catch sight of a Ford Fairmont, puke orange and tan, and break out in goosebumps all over. *It must be him.* My stride starts to come up short, and my head twists as we go by so I can keep looking in the car. "Leslie," my friend says, "what's wrong with you?" But by this time I've looked closely enough to realize that it isn't his. I don't say anything, and look straight ahead.

We all run poorly in the nationals that year, even Kim, who is injured and thinking then about leaving us. By December she does go somewhere else, leaving her place to me. By track season, in spite of the pain I have developed in all my joints and shoulders, I'm running really fast. Track is really my sport anyway. Something about the slide of the curves, the power it takes to make your way down the straight. And the crowd, all gathered in one place, their voices rising, rising, calling my name or any name, just as long as they're standing there to see me.

Cross-country is too spread out, dipped-in curves and tree-lined turns, yards and yards of path where not a soul can see you. In track, all of the focus is on you, and since the events are broken up you're not running in some great big pack. I don't like running with bodies around me, hearing other women's breaths and smelling them, feeling their legs almost touch me. I can't breathe until I've broken into a clear space, where I don't have to see anyone in front of me. For our first home meet Coach Dougherty puts me in the 5,000, even though I'd much rather do the 1,500 or even the 3,000. The 5,000 is the same distance as cross-country, twelve endless laps, and nobody will watch you for all that time, it's too boring. There goes the runner, around and around. So what? I never watch the distance races when I'm not running them, not even the guys'. The shorter stuff is where the power is, but Coach wants me in the longer races, where we're weak. He says I can use my sprinting strength at the end. OK, OK. Some of the crowd who used to follow me in high school shows up, like Coach Estes; I look in the stands and wave.

I play it up in front of the old crowd. I'm proud of my uniform and that I am running with people from South Africa and

Germany and Ireland now. I like being with the team today. My life feels cleaner, battened down, on track. On track like the mechanism of my strides making it around and around these curves so clean, twelve laps and every one right on pace, and when I run by the stands people do cheer me through them all. The announcer makes a fuss about my competition, a woman from UTEP who won the cross-country invitational last fall, but after mile two I don't hear her anywhere near me. Passing the stands, I hear Coach Estes's voice among the others and this makes me smile a little even as I look at the curves and the straights ahead of me really fiercely, even as I concentrate to keep my shoulders forward and my arms loose. Around, around, and I'm breathing easy, feel a whole lot left in me to put into the kick. So 300 yards from the finish I'm up on my toes and fully open, mean, my legs bearing down on the distance like snapping a pencil clean. I finish eighteen seconds ahead of Ms. UTEP Cross-Country. Voices cheer and buzz, but I can hear Coach Estes, clear out from everyone else, yelling, "There she is! That's my girl!"

Machine

It's morning, very early, and the air isn't cold or warm but a little flat. I look at the luminous red numbers telling me it's a bit past four. I nod and press my lips together with satisfaction because I've done it again, woken myself up by the discipline of my internal clock. I don't need any machines, I'm one myself. I sit up and look at one of my roommates, also on the team, sleeping deeply in her bed across the room.

Janine won't get up and she won't be out there this early. This is what makes me different, what sets me apart from her. I'm willing to go to great lengths, and she, well, she, if I could talk about it but out of politeness I don't, is a little lazy, not like me, who survives on six hours of sleep to leave enough time for training and Latin at eight, the time you're always sure to be able to get the class you want because most people are too lazy to get out of bed. My mother keeps asking why I can't be more like Janine, who smiles at my mother and seems happy, talks to her in a pleasant way. "She's balanced, Leslie," my mother says. "You could learn something from her. You're too extreme. Winning isn't everything." I suppress the urge to hit her when she says this.

Why can't my mother get it? Every champion I ever knew of was extreme, and winning *is* everything. Balance is why Janine is a mediocre runner, and she is the last person in the world I want to be like. Balance is why she doesn't get up until seven. At four a.m. you've got the whole world to yourself, it's yours, it's yours, no one else around you to step over or around you or to get in your way and I stretch and punch straight into my leg to make sure it's still hard and glance over at her again.

Breathing, breathing, so much peace. That's exactly what makes Janine happy to be on the second string, to run at the back of the pack every practice, when for me every day is a race, every time I line up with other bodies and fly over the ground. I can't stand to have anyone in front of me, not for a single sprint, not in warmup, not ever. She's happy, and she smiles all the time. She's so normal, so content, but she's a little fatter than those of us in the first string. She's got that extra layer softening her edge and by that you can tell she's not as intense, that she's pretty, she's soft. No one would say Janine's fat, by any means, she's just not like us, stripped down, every fiber out there, twitching, carving, working like a muscle should, carving us a space, getting us noticed.

She trails along and is moral support and no one ever talks to her like she matters. She doesn't because if she didn't go to a meet no one would notice, it would make no difference whatsoever in our scores. She always runs with that pack that's just there, hanging on. I'm not sure why Coach wants them around, those nonscholarship girls who'll never beat us. They go to our workouts just to do it. There's no end, no goal, just improve their own times and I don't get it. Here I am up by exactly 4:06, and I've got myself trained to wake up and do this every day and I move through the perfect, perfect quiet. I'm glad no one else gets up, that every day they tell me, "I don't see how you do it," because it's the way I get ahead and it's so simple, you just get up.

So I head for the stairs, wincing a bit from the pain in my right foot. As I put my weight down I can feel that twinge in my hip but it's all right because it'll go away almost as soon as I start to run. I'm out the door and into that rush of cool air and silence that soak over my skin, for at this hour I've even beat the birds. There's such an extreme hush because there aren't any cars, which usually ride in a solid stream so you get used to the noise like a wall of sound always above you pressing you down. But it's not here right now. The wall has opened up and I can move like silver liquid. I head up the street for the first mile of four and within twenty strides all the pain goes and I am cruising starlight, miles, bigger than my own shadow and stretching out like the expansion of a thousand lungs. I fly and fly and everything else drops away.

About a mile in I stop at the same spot, a flat space of ground under the pine trees by the medical center, a corner just back from the road, out of sight. I drop to the ground and hit my first five hundred sit-ups, my back flat and my hands behind my head, knees raised, lifting my chest enough so my shoulders clear the ground but the small of my back stays in place. I feel that plane of muscle in between my hipbones roll tight and then I concentrate on all the squares that run down the middle. They punch in waves like they're supposed to. It's nice, I can count on it, they always respond. I drop my shoulders, relax half a second.

I'm up and back and at about this point the light has started to lift enough that you can make out the shapes that fall out of the path of the traffic lights. Light lifts enough to wake the doves, and their voices wash over me and the air breathes and I'm up again onto the second leg. It has a stop just like this one at the end of it and I hit five hundred more, and the same happens again on the third and the fourth. By the time I pull back up to those concrete stairs with the shaky railings where the iron shakes and squeaks at every step, I've hit two thousand and my stomach feels toned and tight and my lungs worked up and my legs awake and looking for more.

I give them that later. Now I slip through the sticking, ugly door that sort of grates on the way in and I grab my Latin and put on the water to boil for tea. My roommates won't be up for a long time and I lose myself in declensions for a while and the water boils and I feel the heat of the ceramic cup and hear the hot water soak over the tea smelling of raspberries and lime, and I let it sit until it's very strong and then sweeten it with one pink packet of saccharin I buy in big boxes and the waves of smell and sweetness soothe my head. I forget my foot is throbbing, clean and hot like hungry needles. I forget my hip is more than just a twinge, a pain that sings out clear and bright if I move it, and I let the heat steam over my face and breathe in. I boil another, set a piece of bread in the toaster. I wait one hundred seconds, then pop it out just right, that golden brown that doesn't cry for butter. I get the jar of Smucker's and measure a drop that will cover the bread, give me ten calories more. I bite in. It lasts a while.

I head for the shower and take the stairs one by one, leaning a lot on the rail so I don't have to put too much weight on that hip. I make it down mostly on my good leg and take four Advils right away to dull that pain, shut it up. I make the shower stinging hot but nothing stops the stinging in my foot. It's in the bones of the third metatarsal just under my third toe and as I stand in the heat I can feel it digging at me like I've got spines in there or maybe strips of lead.

I scrub down my hair just the right amount and wait until the rollers are hot. They stay in ten minutes. I touch on a light coat of paint, blend a faint line of blush over the bones along my cheeks, nose, and chin, darken my lashes, brush the curl out, spray it down. Moving slowly, trying to avoid using the hip, I struggle into a short sundress, because though it's only April it's already hot. As I reach back to tie the strings I get a picture in my head of how my back must look, its clean, clean lines, and the cleanness of my legs and I imagine for a minute what my Latin teacher must see when I walk in. I see a steel machine flounced by a dress and who can resist that contrast because my face is soft and beautiful enough and my hair is like rich cotton candy. I feel how the blue strings cross under my shoulder blades, distinct, and I raise my arms flexing the muscle which here at least doesn't hurt. By the time I'm out the door at a quarter till eight my roommates are stirring and I get out quick enough to avoid them, swimming caffeine and endorphins. I try to walk proud but the pain in my foot slows me down.

In Latin sure enough my T.A. looks up when I walk in and he looks at me through lots of declensions. I'm already tan from track work and my hair's bleaching out even a little more white. I look down at my hands, thin like cords of muscle with no protective wrappers, strong hands. I shift my leg, trying not to aggravate that hip, and the muscle curves up nice and the blue skirt rests on it like a gentle hand and as soon as the bell rings I gather my books and try to get up without wincing. I absorb the bright blue shock without showing it on my face; instead I smile and pick up my books and head for the training room across campus.

This early in the morning it's just me and a few of the football players, who are repairing the damage from last fall, trying to catch up before training becomes too intensive this spring. I try to walk straight but it hurts. I find my trainer. His eyebrow twists up, "How is it?" "When I'm running it's fine, it's when I stop." "Well, you don't run all the time." He looks at me as if maybe I do. I look down. "My shoulder's starting to get like the hip, and the pain in the foot isn't better." He says, "You know it won't until you take off more time. I think you should. Remember it's fractured and when you train on it the bones open wider." "Fine," I say, "We've got just another month, it can't get too wide. I can take off a few weeks before cross-country. But why is my shoulder starting to feel like my hip? What can we put on it while I'm in the suds?"

He takes my arm and rotates the bones, and they grind like metal and I wince. "It's bursitis," he says, "just like your hip. I'll give you a cold pack for it while you're in the heat, and then when you're icing your leg we'll give it heat." I shrug my shoulders. "Oh, great, my old favorites, hot and cold. So when will you turn over those drugs?" He grins and pushes my right shoulder, the only part that doesn't hurt. "You'll have to go to Dr. Quack for that—hit the water." I limp to the whirlpool, a vat big enough for twenty bodies. Here I can limp. The pain can show, we all do it. I make a game face, dragging my hip getting in. When I lift it grates like sandpaper over an axle. Laughing, I try to balance legs and heat packs. I look up at the football player across from me, twice as big as me, his leg packed deep in the whirling water.

I ask him, "So why're you in?" and he tells me, "This time it's my knee, it got hit pretty hard and it blew since I planted my foot one direction, got knocked the other." I nod. "That's a little like mine. My foot and hip and now my shoulder. It's the inside leg. It takes most of the weight every turn around the track." He says, "I know, I can feel that in my sprints." We shake our heads and let the heat soak out the pain.

I'm in a long time. I drag myself out and wipe down my leg. The team doctor approaches, looking grave. He rotates my arm around, just as the trainer did, and then my leg, scanning my face for the degree of pain. He nods to himself. He tells me cortisone is the only way to build up the protection around the joints that has been stripped away. It'll cover the bones like a blanket, a coating of oil. I'll finish up practice, the season. Then I can take some time off to rest.

But I can't take time off. I just can't. I think about it as I sit in my car. I head toward practice, and I look down for the tenth time and this time I am sure. My shadow has caught up with me and she's starting to set herself free. She's going to take me over. It's my swollen stomach, yawning like a mouth. All over my legs, big as trunks. I grab a handful of flesh from my thigh. So soft. A sweet sickness twists in my throat, my stomach tightens. It's too loose. It hangs there, dough, like rotting leaves. Fat. I try to straighten a leg out, the one not on the gas. Flex hard. Look. Too much. I know that my thighs touch each other when I stand up. How did this happen? It's the worst in the car. They spread out. They're so big. I pinch them, and something gives. Fat. Dough. There it is.

I've got to do something about this. My stomach is curved. It sticks out. If I go on like this I'll look like them. Like her. Like the lower half of my body is swollen, misplaced. There's this woman on the team. We call her "breadbasket" because her lower abdomen is so swollen and round, sticking out. I can't be her. Not at all. Not one bit. Out of nowhere I think of my mother. Fat at a hundred. Me too. It's what my father would say, "You fat bitch."

I remember looking at her when he says it. Summer and the birds that stop singing, smothered by cotton and everything else I can't hear. It's hot, and it seems like the air conditioner never runs for thrift, so we don't wear a whole lot of clothes. I look at her, draw myself up, curl my lip. My father is right. I look and think, *you're the most disgusting thing I can imagine* when she is sitting down, warm flesh puffing under a halter top she has made herself. There it is. A roll of whiteness mouthing up. This makes me different. No rolls, no rolls, no rolls. *I'm not you I'm not you I'm not you I'm not you who the fuck are you and how can you stand to be so weak and let yourself get like this how can you stand to sit so still why aren't you up why don't you move how can you just let yourself go?* She weighs 100. My father is hard, like a crust. A solid slab, a blackened shape that takes up space. I can't even see her, except the messiness of her lines. Just the puff. I can't breathe. I've got to get out and I run for the fourth time that day, a quick few miles along the darkening street just to make certain I'm solid, my feet can breathe, my stomach is rippling cuts.

Like now, as I head for the track with my cortisoned feet. I can't stop working out, there's no way.

C O W S

For most of this semester I have been so focused. There's only one guy who's been after me, Bernard the pole-vaulter, who—and I am very touched by this—is only after my answers in the sociology class we happen to have together. The way he talks reminds me of the boys in seventh grade who wanted help on their tests and had no interest whatever in my undeveloped breasts. Bernard talks to me like Bruce Candera, that football player in high school I tutored through three years of English essays. After I help him through a couple of soc tests, though, he asks me to dinner to thank me. I figure why not, I'm not doing anything else, and we become a highly unlikely couple after that. But he does have a really nice set of abs, the best I've ever seen. All eight squares out and visible, forget the usual six. And, as a couple of my friends remind me, he looks an awful lot like Conner. Coincidence, surely.

Maybe three-quarters of the way through the season, we fly to Louisiana for a big invitational meet that goes on and on for five days, and Bernard makes a big deal about making sure we sit together on the plane. There are two sprinters on the team who were at Amphi with me; no doubt they try to warn him. I make jabs at him, little sarcastic jokes, in front of the other sprinters; he just smiles at me, doesn't seem to notice. I'm his girl. His girl is in pretty sad shape.

My hips and shoulders have gotten so bad that I really can't walk down stairs without one of my roommates putting her arm around my shoulders or waist and easing me down, and every bone, tendon, and ligament hurts until I start running. After about five miles I am perfectly fine. I can just keep going then. Coach Dougherty told the trainers to prescribe the strongest painkillers for me, and they do take the edge off.

Outside the plane Louisiana comes up humid and hot, making our desert skins swim. The air is so heavy we have some trouble breathing. I feel a little awkward here, sprinters and distance runners all mixed in. The distance girls, five of us, hang nervously together in a pack, plan raids on the 7-Eleven at night when we know Coach Dougherty will be asleep. We walk the mile down the road together and see faces coming toward us, laughing, on the other side of the road. We draw closer together, our skins almost touching. The other group crosses toward us. But it's only our sprinters, with packages of doughnuts they offer us. Oh, no. We're after that trail mix, yogurt raisins coated thick and malt balls and walnuts and pecans. We know how many calories it is. We eat it all in guilt and sin but this time we are in it together: Coach and his handwritten diet sheets have simply become too much. We're breaking out, girls goin' wild.

So tomorrow I get up really early to make sure I can run it off, make sure I can put maybe ten miles in before breakfast since to warm up will take me at least five. Three painkillers first. And out the door into that alarmingly wet air like a slippery skin I'm sucking right into my mouth. It is so quiet right now; everyone else is asleep. I find a trail just to the side of the hotel that wanders back into a fenced-off field. I see the low bodies of cows, moving slowly, like prehistoric dragons in the predawn dark. The smell of timothy, buttercups, so many unidentified scents. There is a fence but I slip through it clean and there are miles and miles of trail that roll out in front of me. I breathe. I watch the cows, they watch me. They clear a path and twitch their tails. Back off just a little, chewing their cuds, curious, kind of nice. I salute them, trundling over the fields. The air's made me loose, I don't hurt much. I get my ten in really smooth, maybe ten minutes over an hour.

Back at the hotel everyone is waking up, scrambling for breakfast and the van. One of the sprinters tells me the pole vaulter's looking for me; I go back for him. Everyone is kind of nervous today, most of us have to run. I don't though, not until tomorrow, and wonder about passing the day. What will I do with myself? Cheer on everyone else? Nah. I've got this book with me, and I ask Coach if it is OK if I don't show up at the track until tonight, claim my hip needs nursing. He agrees, so when we get back to the hotel and everyone else is making their way over to the LSU track, I get *Crime and Punishment* and head back to the field. The cows low at me, greeting me this time. The ground is soft and the grass isn't wet, and the air swims around me like a quiet hand. Timothy, buttercups, floating up. I make myself a place in the field, stretch out to favor the boiling in my hip. One cow comes right up to me, sticking her face into my book. I rub her nose, around her ears. She gives me a rasp of her tongue. It feels so good just lying here. I think of the scenes that must be playing themselves out on the track and shudder. One more race. One more body breathing itself around corners. Start to finish. Again and again. And I am out there the whole day with Raskolnikov and questions of who deserves to die and who deserves to live—only the smartest people deserve to live, he thinks. Ordinary people, like the old woman he kills, are a waste. Every so often I stop reading and look up, so full of these heated words and the feeling of them beating in my blood like bees. I keep stopping to think about Raskolnikov's idea of the elite. It scares me. Sports, competition, me, the other girls . . . the cows low. My hip grinds. I start thinking, *why am I doing this?*

The next day I run the 5,000, and I am really in pain. I'm also scheduled for the 3,200 an hour later. I start to warm up, and the painkillers aren't doing a thing. The pain is back into my foot this time, the bones hot like I've felt before. I know exactly what this is. But my hip grinds, too, my shoulders feel like dried lead. I limp up to Coach Dougherty and tell him it's bad. "Just get through these races," he tells me. "You only have to run today, and we really need the points." OK, OK. I go run three miles to loosen it up. I batten down against the pain, trying to ignore it, but I am still limping to the start when my event is called.

The gun goes off and so do I. Smoother. I'm fine. I take those twelve laps fast, and again there is nobody near me. I win easily, but as soon as I slow past the finish line, the pain is in me like needles pressing everywhere through my feet. My hip like it's come undone.

"Coach," I say, "I can't do the 32. It hurts too much." He is mad. He argues. Pleads with me. Gets mad again. He finally gives up, but his parting shot is to call over to Janine, who has also just finished the 5,000, a minute or more behind me. "Leslie won't run the 32," he says. "She's hurting. But you looked very strong today. We'll have you replace her, all right?"

He knows what this usually does to me, knows it will motivate me to run the race. Like one afternoon a few weeks ago when he made her run with me instead of her usual slower group. He had us start at the same time, but I had to run an 800 while she ran a 600. So by the third one, it was easier for her to keep up with me. I was so mad. He got what he wanted. I ran until the bottoms of my feet were burning that day, until I was sure I would throw up. But now something in me has turned off. It's OK. I don't have to do it. She can have a little of the spotlight, she can run. I'll still be here tomorrow even if I don't.

We get back and the trainers x-ray my foot, which, sure enough, is split down the middle by a stress fracture again. "Well," Steve says, "we can give you enough painkillers to get you through the season. But if you do that, the gap in the bone will open wider and will take much longer to heal. You'll be off most of the summer; if you get off it now, you'll be running again by June."

Coach and I talk, and he pushes for the painkillers, but I decide no. I hurt too much, ashamed as I am to admit it. So I'm back in that pool again, the same place I was last year, except this time I have a better exercise cycle. I don't know it, but my hip all gnarled in the Louisiana heat, flashing Dostoyevski to the cows, is the last time I will travel to a track meet.

Giant

The rest of the season is another endless procession of training room sessions—whirlpool, heat and ice packs, an hour on the training bike, then the whirlpool again, hours put in at the pool. Restless, I break doctors' orders and enter a triathlon but don't even get to the running part because I wreck the bike when I crash it into a guardrail.

Because I have been running less, I calculate, I have to eat almost nothing so I will not put on an ounce of weight. As hard as I ride the training bike or swim, they do not use up the calories the way intense interval training does. I keep looking at my legs in a panic. The one place that keeps tripping me up is a sandwich bar on campus where you can get avocado, tomato, and Swiss cheese with honey mustard on thick wheat bread. I get this every day, even though I know I shouldn't have either avocado or cheese. Too much fat. I love the smell of it as I unwrap it, thick fresh green mixed with deep bread.

I eat my sandwich by myself and go over biology notes. But I eat the one sandwich and can't stop thinking about other food. The afternoon goes on and I think about food during biology lab tapes. The voice on the tape is saying "and paramecium is a subspecies of . . ." and two tapes later, "the pericardium is the membrane on the outside of the heart," and I am trying to take notes but am thinking about the food I can't have, like ice cream and Captain Crunch, that yogurt mix. I think about where I can get them, picture myself getting into my Bug and driving to the right store, where the cashiers won't know me.

My thighs, my knees, my stomach. I examine myself in the mirror every day, piece by piece. I look at everyone else around me, trying to find someone who is thinner. Food crowds out what I learn in classes, sacral and lambdoid sutures, occipital bones in the head, thesis statements of just the right height, and the tenth declension of Latin nouns. Still, without practice, I study fiercely for hours every day, lock myself in the library and copy my notes out in multicolored ink. All the energy I can't put into races I now put into my classes instead. I save my favorite part, my final English paper, for last. It's due at eight the next morning, and it is ten o'clock the night before and I haven't started yet.

So I am gearing up to write. It's on Thomas Mann's *Death in Venice,* a short novel that has moved me like the Dostoyevski—the way it makes you sit still, listening to the beat of your heart in your ears and the way that beat matches the word on the page and suddenly you *know.* The way the book says the things you can't explain to anyone, but you feel them in you, urgent, like another place you have to get to soon, tomorrow or at least by next week. Writing the paper, I know I can explain this. I mark passages and write down some ideas and notice that I'm getting kind of hot. My stomach aches and my mouth is dry from the laxatives I took earlier. The living room in these apartments is upstairs, and I know they haven't turned on the air conditioning yet. It must just be the May heat rising. I get out a fan. But ten minutes later I am shivering cold, and the tips of my fingers are blue. Then blistering hot again, so my brain feels like runny eggs. Some friends from the pool come over, laughing, and I can barely pick up my head, and I don't remember at all what they say except that one of them gets worried and sits down on the couch and holds me in his lap and I am very glad for this because I am going hot and cold all over and am starting to cry because I can't think my head is burning so much and my bones are aching, the fire is in them like thousands of stress fractures everywhere, turning them inside out.

When I try to get up I am so stiff I can't move and I cry but I laugh and people are there and then it is quiet and they are not. At two a.m. the fever flees, replaced by a low-grade heat and this aching. I am empty of everything, whatever it was that just burned wild through me, left me tired and weak, but my head is clearer. I sit down with *Death in Venice* and write from that cleared space, the sweat that comes after the fever, and by eight a.m. I am sure I have found it, some secret I had no way of speaking about before this. I make my way to campus to turn in my fevered words.

Inside out, what a sight I must have been. The teaching

assistant looks at me with his eyebrows raised, almost asking if I'm OK. Starts to form the words, then thinks better of it, maybe. It's enough. Flushed with whatever that precious insight was, giddy with fever, the impression on me is that I've been seen.

Is he fascinated by me, does he want to touch me or listen to me speak? Beautiful wreck. My new look, maybe. But maybe he isn't looking at me at all. Maybe the careful look I get has to do with the fact that I am still shaking, my skin is still blue, and I smell of laxatives and heavy sweat.

That night is the first of an ongoing series of attacks, which happen more often and get worse each time. But I just sweat them out and ignore them—they go away in twelve to twenty-four hours, nothing to worry about. I push my training a notch higher to make up for it. Catching up, catching up, trying to make up for lost time.

The summer of 1983 is rough, but I am at my fanatical best. I get up at five and run ten miles, do a thousand-plus sit-ups under the apricot trees. Some days I do just a thousand; some days I challenge myself and do more, and then the next day I have to do more than that just to stay ahead. But I have only so much time: my mother sticks her head out the back door some mornings to ask why I need to do so many and to tell me it's getting late. I eat some shredded wheat and then bike to the pool, this year a good fifteen miles away. I teach swimming lessons all morning, then run a three-miler on lunch break. Lifeguard all afternoon, then ride my bike to the weight room at the university. Lift hard, especially legs. I bike the extra ten miles home, have something small for dinner, put in another quick four-mile run. I go to bed by eight and am up at five.

One morning I do a ten-miler and start to feel pretty stiff at the end. I'm also really hot and take my temperature, thinking I might be getting the flu. It's a 102, but I'm stiffening up so fast it's getting hard to bend my fingers and the thermometer falls out of my hand. I draw a hot bath, thinking that might loosen me up, and by now I'm starting to get chills too. Burning and freezing at the same time, I lower myself into the water. It's hot, but the bones start to feel a little loose. I sit there until the heat drains away and then make a move to rise. Nothing happens. I get my hands on the side of the tub and try again. My fingers are so stiff that I slip. I try to move to my knees but it hurts too much to bend anything. I start laughing. I can't move. I can't get myself out of the tub. I try again but slip and hit my head this time. I call for my mother.

I'm so stiff by this time she can barely pull me out, and I can't stop laughing. I have no control over my body and there is something really hysterical about this. "What is wrong with you?" she keeps saying. "You just can't keep training as hard as you do. You're not a steamroller, Leslie. You are not some goddamn machine." Background noise, static, she has said this before. She will say it again.

Twelve aspirin later I am back at the pool, only two hours late for work. The fever has broken and I've loosened up and just feel a little weak maybe, like something's burned through and left me quiet and cold. And by noon I'm feeling good enough to do my normal "A" mountain routine.

This year I'm at this pool in the heart of the barrio, Menlo Park, because Jacobs, the pool across from the high school where I guarded last year, is closed for updating and repairs. A group of us from that pool are shifted to Menlo, at the base of one of Tucson's most infamous hills, "A" mountain, which stands out from the rest of the landscape like a clean limb. Kids do drugs on those hills in their low riders at night, rumor has it, but during the day, it is only a shimmering monument in the heat, too hot for anyone to brave it. You can see the "A" marking it from every freeway surrounding the town. Menlo nests at the base of it, a few residential neighborhoods underneath, in the center of a park, where the walls to the changing rooms are scrawled with graffitti, CINDY & JOE, and different gang names written on top of each other, trying to claim the most space. White kids guarding at a barrio pool, we've been warned to look out for *mexicanos* with numbchucks, and I think about Ray, who always had a set along with him at Peña Blanca Lake. He just had fun with them. But we are instructed that they are weapons and to look out for them and even, it is kind of whispered, to look for guns. If we see anything like this, we are supposed to call the police. But we never have to. Mostly there are just these sweet neighborhood kids and the kids that have followed us from the other pool.

Usually the first swimming lesson starts at seven, the heat already so sharp it made your chest ache, and today is the first lesson I've ever missed. Usually at seven there's the buzz of cicadas, and the temperature's up to 108. Kids and kids, night water, skin chilled to a prick, bodies bright from the height of a dive. Shriek and splash, grins, eyes. Margie and Michael, my favorite twins, bursting in through the gates every morning shouting my name and their fates and their activities of last night and *come on already let's get in the pool,* gawky bodies. Then shy and silent children holding onto my hand, eyes brown with fear and tugging back, please do I have to go in, taken aback by disregardful twins, throwing themselves through airy space, never looking behind, never looking to see what would find them.

All morning easing children into the water, teaching them to breathe and to stroke, turns into lunch hour, where some of the other lifeguards head out to the Eegee's to bring back food but I always head out for the mountain, and in spite of the weirdness of this morning I decide to go again today. The guys I work with don't know what to do with this. I use it to show them, put brackets around their flirtations with me, just so they know they have to take me seriously. I am glad that by now it's 110, that while everyone else is inside in the shade, I am braving it. I start running and five minutes into it, beet red and sweating, I have changed into a giant. A furnace fire in my chest, I climb slower and slower up the radical hill, my steps a thunder. The sweat so sweet, my legs so hard, so strong. Nothing to stop me. Not a thing. I am the only one who can do this, who *does it*. One of the guy lifeguards decides one day he will try it with me and makes it only a fourth of the way to the top until he turns. But I take that hill easily, day after day. I'm revved.

Captain Crunch

I allow myself one shift from routine and go to Phoenix to stay with Janine. Most of the shift she is working, eight hours, I spend taking aerobics classes at the gym. I do five in a row and then lift. Still a little time left, so while she is gone I also do the kind of eating I do in secret, away from everyone else, the kind of food I would never let anyone know I touched. I stop at the grocery store, looking carefully around me to make sure no one notices. I get a half gallon of ice cream, turtle fudge, and the family-size box of original Captain Crunch. I throw some Raisin Bran and bananas into the cart just so it doesn't look strange. I am nervous at the checkout line and don't look the cashier in the eye. I wonder if the person behind me knows. The air feels full of tension as I wait for the bill. I pay cash and walk quickly away, breathing out and feeling lighter, but all I can think of is the food, of putting it in my mouth. And once I have started like this I don't stop.

I tear open the Captain Crunch as soon as I get to the car, start throwing it down in handfuls with the hand that isn't on the wheel. I am not savoring the taste of the sugar in my mouth or eating it because I am hungry. I am blank, mechanical, consuming it fist over fist. My head is empty of everything except eating, like a kind of sleepwalking or trance. I walk into Janine's empty house and go right to the family room, where they have just gotten MTV. This is its second season and I have never seen it before, and I am watching the images in the same way I eat, not stopping, not thinking. I turn it on and sit down, eating the ice cream right out of the carton, as fast as I can without the cold freezing up my head. Mouthful after mouthful. I am vaguely aware that my stomach is starting to hurt, fill up. I keep chewing, blank, nothing more in my head than those Louisiana cows had when they stood next to me while I was reading beside them in their field, chew, and chew, and chew. Just the motion of it, I can't really taste anything. I keep going until the carton's empty, then make the bologna sandwich that I would never otherwise eat, with some mayonnaise even. By now I am nauseous, my stomach packed tighter than a swollen cat. I get out a hand towel and a stadium cup full of water. I drink about a third of it, tie my hair back, get down on my knees in front of the toilet. The water makes everything come up easy, and I stick my index finger down my throat so that it does. Ice cream is the easiest thing to throw up, especially if you get it right away. I don't gag, really; my stomach muscles tighten just like they do in a sit-up, and everything comes up really smooth, even the sandwich, which, since it is the last thing I have eaten, comes up first. It gets harder as you go along; you have to drink more and more water each time.

I keep sticking my finger down, carefully wiping it off, until I get nothing several times so I know that I am clean. I wipe the toilet, flush, rinse the towel. I drink another cupful of water so I won't get dehydrated, a little Gatorade so my electrolytes won't get unbalanced. And because I have read that the residue of stomach acid from throwing up like this can wear down the enamel on your teeth, I brush them clean.

I wash the the spoon carefully, then put it away. I crush the cardboard containers and bury them underneath the garbage beneath the sink. I keep watching MTV, even after Janine gets home. We scan the women's bodies, commenting on whether they are fat, whether or not they are in as good shape as we are. Most of them, we decide, are not, for even if thin they are flabby, whereas we are tight and smooth. We should be on MTV, we joke. Why don't they come looking for us, the female athletes, who have better bodies than anyone? That night we go see *Flashdance,* a movie about a dancer who overcomes her no-count trailer park life because of the way her body looks and her dedication to her dancing, which get her a great role in a big dance production as well as a rich man. The way she dresses in that movie is the way everyone at the gym has been dressing.

Now we see why. Sweatshirts torn to give a glimpse of a body worked out tight. Showing your skin, but something stronger than that, too—your body shaped into an achievement, sort of, this thing you have managed to create, so it protects you from being *just* sexual or cheap. Being sexual without being cheap. That night, we both take the scissors to our Arizona T-shirts, cutting off the neck and arms, tying what were the armholes low near one shoulder so our collarbones show. We also cut the bottom into sections, cuts down both sides and a slit up the back and the front, then another knot in both places. Women wear their shirts like this all summer and through the next fall, showing off.

A couple of weeks before the fall semester, Coach Dougherty and the men's coach take both teams to cross-country training camp in the woods of northern Arizona. We stay in facilities that are set up for a kid's camp, the ones you go to when you are ten, cabins with cobwebs in the corners and narrow, narrow sets of bunk beds, concrete floors, and only one dim mirror in the bathroom. With so many people around, it's hard to find time this week to throw up, and I do it less. To many people's surprise, except Coach Dougherty's and mine, on the very first run we all take as a group I am so far ahead of the other women I am actually running in the tail-end group with the men. Of course I have done this before, but that was high school, when anyone can do a thing like that, and this is NCAA Division I. I repeat this enough throughout the week that eyebrows are rising all around, my God, look at Heywood cranking. So the ranks for the season are set in place, and I am unquestionably first.

A week after we get back Coach Dougherty calls me and asks if, as the number one runner, I will pose for the cross-country publicity poster with the number one guy runner. We go to Reid Park to shoot this, where we run our at-home meets. A photographer takes frame after frame, mostly with us running toward him, and then the photo is converted into a computer graphic of the two of us in red and blue, a little flesh-tone shaded with dark patches for our muscles, hair, and skin. ARIZONA over the top of our heads and CROSS-COUNTRY across our bodies, the graphics of the letters and the fluid patches of our bodies say power. Our names are spelled out in small letters down in the corners next to our lower legs, showing who we are is less important than the general message, but I don't care.

I have been chosen to stand for Arizona cross-country, and a feature article early in the season presents me as the number one runner. SHE RUNS "A" SLOPE BECAUSE IT'S THERE the headline says, over a shot of me taking "A" mountain in my flashdance shirt, my face bleached beautiful and blank. *"You can have it all,"* the article says, and for all anyone knew, my life says it too.

B l o o d   t o   a   G h o s t

Except there are two faces in the pictures, two different girls. One is the bright, hopeful, all-American kid, a girl in ways that are clean. Just a small touch of ruggedness, sweet curiosity, a touch of derring-do. She has her hair-bows tied just right and a smile that beams out at you, clear. By her side is just the right guy, strong-jawed and patrician, button-down oxford and Bass Weejuns, class valedictorian white. In her senior picture, she looks really young, more fourteen than seventeen, hair pulled back from her face with a vaguely haunted, crooked-mouth smile that looms a little larger on the right side. Her face is an oval, chin tapered to a perfect point, her forehead smooth. Her chin rests on her arms, white strands of hair filtering around her face. Even her eyes don't quite give pause, the right size for her face and a bright clear blue, black lashes carefully separated and curled. *I'm doing it,* the eyes say, *and I have pulled it off, too, don't you see my refinement and grace? Just look at the smooth lines of my cheek, the way my neck sweeps into my shoulder. See how gentle I am, smooth as an Easter egg whose yolk has not quite cooked. See the softness of my lips, the way only gentleness passes between them. Quiet things. Good things. See? I am your precious, precious little girl, your dear heart, lovey-dove. Your sweetness. My skin so clear, so white, no mark on it. Dear girl. You would hold me in your arms, against your chest, smoothing my eyelids with your thumbs. Precious child. Your arms. I am the one who lay still for you, remember? Why don't you want me? Oh, to put myself in someone's arms and have him hold me like a baby bird with stumps instead of feathers, a while away from growing wings. But something's wrong with me.*

Hard on the heels of the first girl is the second, just a little too sexy to be clean. Suggestive. She's the runner, but something in her is not solid, quite; she beckons you to take her into your mouth like a piece of cotton candy, maybe. Except for the eyes. Her eyes ruin the suggestiveness, get it wrong. She is in her lifeguard bathing suit at the pool, a red lycra Arena, modestly cut. It's the way she's leaning that does it, the angle of the head, how her hands lie next to her hips. Long nails, one leg slightly in front of the other, the bones of her shoulders just the slightest bit sloped. *Come in.* But the eyes, which are hard to make out in the photo's bad light, still have way too much expression to work. With that much sadness, this invitation is a terror, the body shouldered as if it doesn't know. Insensible.

I get Bernard to come up to my house one day, take shots of me in different poses, a bad in-home version of something like *Glamour Shots.* Why do I want this? But I do, and he obliges. Most of them came out blurred, overexposed. Hair up, dressed in a black halter dress. Wrapped in a towel, languishing in the doorway to my sister's bedroom. Full body shots in a pink bikini. And the most frightening one in a one-piece black maillot, cut low in the front and deep into the sides, black with large spots of orange-red and purple-blue breaking it up. There she is again. Next to the pool, her left leg lifted onto a white wire chair, her left hand resting on her thigh. The point is to show off her leg. The hair all long and curled into its frizzy float, sweeping below the shoulders, perfectly manicured hands, bare feet.

But this time her eyes are closed, and there is something clearly wrong with her face. Burned too red, for one thing, its oval like a fierce heart. The mouth slightly open, a dark line between the lips. High cheekbones. But with the eyes closed like that, the bones look swollen, pained. Aged. The mouth suggestive not of sex but pain, as if she were standing there holding every breath in just waiting for whatever it is that's about to hit. A swollen sleeping beauty, some mask settled down on her face. The year I am a babe I am bulimic. The year I am a babe I am an exercise freak, the number one runner on the team. Number one babes have no lines down their faces. Number one babes don't cry out and show pain. But it's catching me. It's starting to show on my face.

The Wake

Number one runner, whose body is breaking up. It's getting harder and harder to lead the workouts each day, and the joint-fever attacks are coming faster and faster, fierce storms that for two or three days sometimes keep me from running. I hold my place in the first couple of meets, but each practice I feel weaker and it's getting harder to hold on. Now when I reach for the roaring inside, the place that holds all my energy and speed, nothing happens. On the week of the Pac-10 Conference meet held in Tucson that year, on our home course, on Halloween, I have had two attacks already. I feel like my insides are all sucked out, my hands and lungs both weak. There will be a huge crowd there, all the coaches and teams from the local high schools, and they'll be watching for me to see how their home girl is faring with the big girls, whether or not Leslie Heywood can still hold her own in college. I can't. No amount of will's going to make me faster this week and maybe not many other weeks soon. I decide the only way to avoid humiliation is to make them not see me. I know people pick me out by my hair, so claiming it's part of a costume for a party I have to go to right after the meet, I dye my hair black. This way I'll run right by and no one will know that Heywood has choked.

The gun goes off and I surge ahead, run strong for the first mile. There are maybe ten runners in front of me, and black dye starts to streak down my face with the sweat. It gets in my eyes and makes them tear. I try to keep running the same pace, but women are passing me, and as much as I try to dig deeper my legs and arms start to harden. Stiff as a graveyard monument, I break into goose bumps and then sweat dye into my uniform in a spreading stain. I am still running, but slower and slower now, barely able to hold a place mid-pack. Since no one calls my name when I run by I know the disguise has worked, and I am glad for it. I finish somewhere in the middle, in thirty-third place.

I have already told Coach Dougherty what is happening to me but he says I have to run and I know he's suspicious that I'm just looking for an excuse to wuss out. The team doctor looks at me and runs some tests but he says everything is fine. He tells Coach it is psychosomatic, probably, that I'm imagining it, and suggests the same thing to me.

After a couple months of this I go to my family doctor, who happens to be a competitive runner, too. I've seen him at a lot of the local road races, out of his white coat looking like all the other skinny guys who run distance—like a scarecrow in nylon briefs. At first he can't find anything either, but I don't feel that he thinks I am making it up. "I need to see you when you have an attack," he tells me. "Whenever it is, call me, and I'll come in."

After the team's poor showing at the conference meet our season is over, and I'm trying to stay on top of the game. There's a local road race on a Saturday, a half-marathon, 13.1 miles. I enter, thinking it'd be good to see how I fare at this distance. Most of the road races I've run have been shorter, and I want to see if I can win at this. I feel a tap on my arm at the starting line; it's my doctor, who smiles and wishes me luck. He takes off at a fast pace and I'm pacing myself because I'm not sure how I am at this distance. So I don't see him for quite a while after the start. But at mile ten I've opened up and am feeling very strong. I pick off pack after pack of tired men; as far as I know the women are all behind me. The men tend to straggle in a line, and there's a skinny guy running ahead of me tight. I pass by easily, but coming up on his shoulder I realize it's my doctor. I raise my hand as I go by, gunning for the next set of runners a few hundred yards ahead.

I win the women's division easily and have been done for a couple of minutes when he finishes. I see him cross the line then disappear into the crowd. A few minutes later I'm getting dizzy. I stay for the awards ceremony, but I'm having a hard time seeing right because I have a high fever. By the time I get home the stiffness has set in and I'm moving really slowly. My puppy whines outside, and I don't have the strength to open the back door and let him in. I make it to the phone, and one of my friends drives me to the emergency room, where they call my doctor, catching him on the way home from the race.

I'm conscious enough to grab *Finnegans Wake* on the way out so I'll have something to read. I want to be sure not to lose any time. I'm sitting on the hospital bed, fever burning the back of my eyes, waiting for someone to come and do something. I read the first few pages again and again but can't understand a word of it. I wonder if it's the writing itself or the fever, because my eyes are so hot it's getting hard to see.

My doctor comes in. "Well," he says, joking, "This is what you get for beating me in the race. You'll think twice about it next time." I can still move my mouth and laugh; I try to lift my arm, in its usual attack-catatonic state, and tell him "I'm not running anywhere just now." "Yeah, I can see that," and the joking stops.

He does tests on me while I lie there, unable to move. After the fever, I am freezing. My hands get blue and so cold it is clear the blood has stopped running through them, and the same thing happens in my feet. My body temperature drops several degrees. At home when this happens, ten layers of comforters and blankets can't console me; here I have only a blanket. I swing wildly from 96 up to 103, and I lose sense of everything except what is directly in front of my face.

The same minute seems to happen over and over again. Sweat soaks the mattress through the sheets. I stiffen up so much I can't hold onto my book because of the way the joints in my fingers swell up. I can't bend my arms or knees. A nurse comes in to help me roll to the side.

Just another day at the OK Corral. This happens so often now I know I can no longer keep up. I can't keep running harder, because there are so many days I'm like this I'm tired all the time. It's like running along the edge of a cliff where the ground keeps crumbling right under your feet so that every step you take forward is followed by a slip and you have to pull back just to keep yourself up.

For six months I've been laughing when I get immobilized like this because the attacks always pass so quickly. I can be ironic and joke, *here's the great runner, reduced to the shininess of fevers, could you just brush my teeth a little bit for me, please? Don't feel quite up to that particular feat today.* I can laugh because the next day it all goes away and I can do everything at the same level.

But that's changing. Like a car that's been running in fifth gear for years, something in me is shutting down. I know it. I can feel it coming the way you feel the air shake when a plane is beginning its final descent.

Break On Through

The tests my doctor does on me go on for several months. We're between track and cross-country seasons, so I don't have to run with the team very often. Coach Dougherty and the team doctor still suspect me of faking it because I can't take the pressure. In early January, just before the spring semester and track practice start, my doctor calls me in. I have been waiting for his answer as if he is a translator who can decode this map in a foreign language I have found that will direct me to the next place I need to go. I'm called into his office rather than an examination room. It looks like a psychiatrist's office, with its oriental rugs and leather sofa, the polished dark wood of the desk. It has a big window and there is a huge saguaro directly outside, its arms jutting toward us.

"You'd better sit down," he tells me. "I know what is wrong with you now," and though I like him a lot I am thinking *he knows what is wrong with me? Seems I've heard ideas about that somewhere before. Now would that be the body or the mind, doctor, or maybe my heart? The part that some people call the soul?* but he is saying that as a runner he knows what it is to have to run and that he has a friend, a psychiatrist, who has treated other people with these things, and he will make sure his friend can see me because I am going to need it. It's cold today and unusually for Tucson it is gray and I'm looking from the window and the way the gray looks cold on the saguaro outside then back to his face, thin and earnest, looking straight at me like you would look at a dog you can't quite trust to keep calm or a kid you have to tell that her favorite pet has to be put down for rabies. He is looking at me almost as if he wants to hold onto my hands but he doesn't.

Instead he is speaking, trying to put medical language into words that make sense and he is talking about immune system disorders and lupus and says I have some version of these things, a version that, because it combines symptoms of several disorders, is called mixed connective tissue disease. It comes from extreme stress. "Your body is attacking itself," he says. "Instead of attacking a virus or infection that comes in from outside, your immune system is attacking all your own joints. It's done some damage. You're nineteen, right?" I nod. "Well, your joints think they're fifty. The attacks wear them down and if the stress load continues, the attacks will spread. Your immune system will eat up more than joints."

My doctor's trying to get eye contact now so I look at him. He looks so sincere, kind of cute. I wonder briefly if he is married, but a word catches my attention and I focus on the words instead of his mouth. "Unless something changes, your immune system will eventually start attacking your vital organs," he says. "You know—your liver? Your heart?" and I am looking at him just listening. "Leslie, you have to stop competing."

At first the meaning does not sink in. I start to speak. "OK, I can probably redshirt track season this spring, and then I'll have a year of extra eligibility past senior year and that will give me some extra time . . ."

He cuts me off. "No. Not a semester. Probably years. You won't be able to train at the same level of intensity ever. I know how hard this is going to be for you, but you have to listen to me and you should go talk to my friend. I know what this must sound like to you. I know you feel like you have to run. But you're going to have to find other things to focus on. I know how difficult this is going to be, but there are other things. You don't have a choice. It's going to get worse if you don't stop. Your immune system will start attacking your heart, and then . . ."

He draws his hand across his throat for emphasis, black humor, laughing a little with his mouth, but his eyes are deadly serious. Then his mouth settles, too, and his eyes look worried. "You can't compete anymore. You're going to have to do something else."

No more steamroller, no machine. My mother was right: I'm just a girl after all. I can't hack it. I go through half an hour of buts and what ifs, but my doctor is convincing. I'm through.

I walk out of the office with a hole whistling through my gut like the wind outside, whipping hair against my mouth and sticking in my teeth. I sit in my car for a minute before turning the key. *They were right. I guess I'm not worth much of anything, really. Not so tough.*

I pull my hair straight back from the scalp and tighten the rubber band. I take it out and pull it tighter. I watch the windshield wipers clear the rain, rub across the bones of my face. Back and forth. The rain hits. I close my eyes. There's something in my throat, and then my mind jumps to where I'm numb. Numb, but the emptiness I am feeling has a lightness to it. More than just fear. The emptiness is also relief.

So what do you do, exactly, when your doctor tells you, "That's it, soldier, you're out of the war"? Like returning from a trip to find you no longer have a house, my world is gone from me, *place, marking, bones, teeth. The reason for strength in my legs and the kind of shoes that I wear on my feet. The kind of "I am" in the back of the throat like a light, the reason to eat, not eat, to breathe, to stretch, to think.* All that is left is the rest. I should walk slowly that first week, but I don't, for I am losing time now and there has to be another way.

There isn't. I emerge from running like someone too long underwater. I have to learn to breathe again, to see everything around me, the terrible blue of a late desert sky, the way the rocks buckle down into the cliffs. The way a person's face moves when she speaks. All this has been covered by this mile and that rep and the ones behind them, like in those running-shoe ads meant to be inspiring. There a thin woman runner is photographed from behind, her long, straight hair in a ponytail so you can see the muscle definition in her shoulders and back, the smooth thinness of her endless legs, one foot in front of the other in the middle of nowhere, just going, nothing around her, running toward a sign that says "road never ends."

But it does end. I have to stop. I have to get used to the idea that people aren't going to stop me in the grocery store to ask me about my running. That I won't be recognized in many places, or any place at all. That I'll be just *some girl*.

When track practice was right after English class on Mondays, Wednesdays, and Fridays freshman year, I used to walk into class dressed in my running shorts, new Nike spikes slung over my shoulder. Someone always asked me about training, about the season, would say they had seen me in the paper that day.

Now I would walk into a classroom and everyone's eyes would slide by without stopping, the teacher's voice running over my name without a ripple of recognition. No more "aren't you the runner who . . ." or "so when's your next big race?" It lasted only as long as I could keep doing it. In a moment I have gone from a visible presence to a ghost, transparent, no density at all. No more Leslie the track star. One of those puffer fish that has nothing inside, pick me up and blow through me like you'd blow through the candles on a cake.

When I have to stop competing, my scholarship is cut in half, and then it is cut completely. I have to make money, and I want to stay in shape. I apply to teach high-impact aerobics at the club and am put on the substitute list. This means I can be called in to teach a class at any time. Right after I'd just thrown up, maybe. If that happens, I'll be too tired and swollen to teach. It will show. In my shiny purple unitard, the straight line of my torso will be disfigured by a bulge.

The only way to get my own class, a permanent gig, is to be available from six in the morning until ten at night, seven days a week. Workouts don't stop for weekends: I'm on call at all times. I want that job. I need it, a place where people still follow me, where I'm the head of the pack. I stop throwing up and start eating enough to be able to pace myself through teaching four or five classes a day. They call me the general.

Apocalypse Then

Fifteen years later I'm still waiting for a mission. Sometimes I'm Martin Sheen trapped in that hotel room at the beginning of *Apocalypse Now*, jumping at enemies who aren't there, collapsing when there's nothing to fight. I've drawn the line at smashing mirrors and smearing myself with my own blood, but some dishes have been sent to an early grave and the quick way my tone turns to anger, or my intensity on the Stairmaster, are sometimes out of place. Everything feels too small. When the walls close in, I head to the gym, where I can stomp and conquer and it won't seem completely out of place.

The gym is packed with bodies. A prerecorded dance tape plays over the speakers. There are aerobics classes in two rooms, and boxing in another. The free-weight space is on the far wall, then circuit equipment, then cardio machines.

My own little war zone. I put on a good scowl. In the other bodies, moving from weight rack to weight rack, machine to machine, I see the enemy, looking at me like I'm just a girl, waiting to take me down. I prowl around, on guard, *just try to make me move out of your way. Just try to question my right to be here.* But they never question it. They get out of my way. Come on, you wussies. You could give me more of a fight. But behind that fierce face I crank into, I'm a little glad I don't have to fight.

The times, they are a-changin' . . . enough girls play sports now that people have been studying female athletes and asking questions about girls like me. The other day I read a government report about us, the first of its kind, while I was on the Stairmaster. In my bra top and sweats, pen in hand, glasses foggy, triceps and quadriceps holding me up so I could move my legs fast enough while marking the important places, I read it straight through. Strange to see these words about yourself, your ghosts, your days, your fiery dreams, all sealed up in a report. Your story, with its guts missing. No smell of fear. No burning lungs from one too many sprints. No shouting voices, the blood's rush through the temples, just words. Sweating, turning the pages, still doing a form of it, I learned the name for what I had: *female athlete triad:* eating disorders, exercise compulsion, leading to amenorrhea, loss of bone. It is good to have names. It is good to know that others have lived your craziness.

But I wondered about what had gone missing, all the things the report didn't say. None of the words told me too much about why any of us get this. Why some of us cross over a line that kicks us free of the earth and into a space where there is nothing, literally nothing, but reps and sweat and improving your times, and why for others sports is a shining thing that gives them blood and a backbone that holds them up, makes them part of this world, wide awake and ready for more. I've lived both places.

Is whatever put me at risk for female athlete triad the same thing that makes me look at the female athletes on television and in magazines with a little bit of sadness today? Because the more of us there are around, the less unusual I will be. No more colorful exotic bird, her muscles and strength her special plumage. One of a crowd. But the town where I live hasn't caught up to the rest of the world yet. I'm still special. Still a big fish in a small pond, in a place where there's few women who are really serious yet. So some people, like the woman who spoke to me out of nowhere in the locker room, think I am heroic. "My boyfriend thinks you're amazing," she says. "You walked by him on the treadmills yesterday, and he said he automatically felt like he had to straighten up, get tough." Some people, like my nonathletic, intellectual friends, think I am pathetic—*can't you see how you're still caught up in that power thing, manipulated and controlled by how you look?* I know, I know, but it makes me feel good. I don't know how I will feel when—as will certainly happen—there are women all around who are just like me.

For now, I can laugh at myself just a little about how tiny my wars are, that no one else even knows they're being fought or whether or how they're won. It's how I keep from collapsing, and the gym, not the track, is my home now. I love striding to the weight tree and grabbing the 45-pound iron plates, the ones that the big boys use, swinging that plate up to the bar as casually as swinging a towel. On the bench, 185 slides up easy, my chest tight as a drum when I pump it up. On good days, with a spotter, I can get 210.

Each new set makes me feel I am there in the room, further and further each time. No one can mess with me. No one can tell me to go away. No one can tell me I'm too loud or I push too hard. It happens for all of us clanging the free weights: we get visibly bigger each set. Each set we get warmer, our muscles tighten with blood, the lines of our bodies fill out tight. You can see clefts between our shoulder muscles, tight rounds of biceps and hamstrings, smooth plates of our stomachs and chests. Each rep. *Yes. Here I go. Here's one for all the times someone told me a girl should be feminine and petite, that I'd better watch out or I'd get too big. Here's another for each time I spoke or screamed and my voice spun through the air like dust. And here's my last tortured rep for those who said they could love me if only I could be just a little bit nicer and quieter, please, not quite so intense. Here we go, 205 to the sky: feel much better already, baby.*

I don't have a runner's body. I don't weigh 110 anymore—I weigh close to 150. Of course I must insist that no more than twelve percent of that is fat, and that I am built for strength and density now, not luminosity and speed. Once in a while, I still worry that this way of thinking is just an excuse, trying to make do with second best because I failed at the stick-thinness thing. I still worry about my stomach, keep a vigilant watch over my thighs. No major disaster has happened yet.

It took me fifteen years to stop panicking whenever I got on the scale. Now I can look at 148 without cringing, though weighing in at the doctor's office is still something I dread. Once a gynecologist told me I weighed too much for my height. Then she looked at my biceps and said, "Oh, you're a bodybuilder. I'm sorry. These charts don't fit you." *Nope, I am another breed entirely, baby.*

The guy who trains me for power lifting tells me a few of his female clients say they want to tone up but they don't want to get as big as that woman he trains. You know, the professor? But just a few of them, he reassures me. Just a few. I remember when I didn't want to be this big, either. I was afraid of taking up too much space.

I'm not now. Movements sharp, head up, shoulders back, eyes straight ahead, *I am I am I am I am* so you might as well go ahead and look. Pan back a little and it might look silly—*yeah, you've got some biceps—so what?* But pan in a little closer and you might begin to notice other things. Like that for years, I was the only girl who walked this way: it was a *guy thing.* Not now. More and more women are walking as if they've got a right to be there, and like the men, their bodies aren't perfect either.

Recently, riding the bike in the middle of the cardio machines, my Walkman on, I saw a woman come out of the punching-bag room after going a few rounds with the gloves. Middle-aged, ordinary looking, just a hint of biceps, she walked the way I do, right down the floor, right by everyone sweating and treadmilling, biking away. Our eyes met; she saw I had seen and we nodded our heads to each other and smiled.

She walked that way out of the building and straight out into the world, upstate New York on a November Sunday, falling leaves in the air, the sky threatening rain.

She walked out and the Boy Scouts walked in. Maybe seven years old, a twelve-boy pack, flanked by fathers and troop leaders, some with their scout scarves on and some with the of-the-moment shirts proclaiming NO FEAR, in they trooped. Their eyes opened wide: the machines, the treadmills, rows of bikes, and me. I couldn't help but smile as they kept staring (*you've got better arms,* a gym old-timer had told me the day before, *than most of the guys in here*), looking away quickly when I caught them, their eyes wide and hungry, not for me but to be me. Hungry, the way I always look at Arnold Schwarzenegger, wanting not him but to be him.

But there are some ways that Arnold wasn't the best model. Ways that the things that most tore me up came from acting like the vibes Schwarzenegger sent: *I am invulnerable. There is no one else around me.* The isolated hero, conquering the world. By herself. All or nothing. Win or lose. Everyone around her an enemy. Like running headlong down a street marked NO OUTLET, I competed so fiercely it was part of my every waking thought. Lately, after years of trying not to compete, being told not to, I've had to admit it's in me like my arteries and veins. I can't not do it. So I've been trying to imagine other ways to do it than the way I always have.

I've had some serious practice. It's gray, it's November, and I'm at a gym in Utica, New York for a power lifting meet. The parking lot is over-full. I walk in the door, trying not to be nervous, trying not to care whether there will be any competitors who can challenge me. People greet me as I walk in the door: "Leslie! How're you doing? What're you opening with today?" I get several slaps on the back in my passage.

My face flushes from the recognition. Like my track days, here is a place people know me. Here is a place people care. But just a few minutes later, the whispers start. There is a new girl at the contest today, her opening lift almost as high as mine. She's been winning contests all over the state. "Sheila's her name," several people tell me. "She's over there," and they point.

I look across another small knot of women whose faces I know, and they look at me and smile, their hands raised in greeting. I walk over to them and they move their circle out a little to let me in. "What've you been up to? How's your training going? I'm opening at 100 today, up 20 from last time. What about you?" We all talk comfortably, no one nervous. "You heard about Sheila?" someone says. "Looks like you'll have some competition today."

I look at Sheila, by herself in the corner in a real power lifter's suit, its tight blue casing around her legs, the top not on yet. Half-consciously I adjust the strap of my own cotton bra top. A power lifter's shirt is made of nylon and so tight that when you put it on, your arms stand out straight before you like Frankenstein's monster striding out looking for kids. Wearing one of those shirts separates the men from the boys, the recreational lifters from the real thing. I don't have one.

Sheila is looking down and stretching against a bar, her

mouth moving just a little as if repeating something to herself. She doesn't look up. Every few minutes her trainer, a short, broad man with powerful shoulders and hips, comes over and pats her on the back, issuing instructions. They are taking this very seriously. I don't have any trainer but myself.

Probably I can't match up to this, me without a bench shirt and with no real training. My hero's egotism: on one level, because no one usually is even close to me, I hadn't thought anyone would be today. I start to get a little nervous, that old unsteady mix of dread and aggression, arrogance and fear, that had always pumped my prerace heart. Pounding again, a little bit alive again. I toe the gym's rubber floor, and the announcers begin to call for the opening weights. The women around me wish me and each other good luck, touching each other on the arms. Except for Sheila in her corner.

Some time passes before anything gets underway. I feel the restlessness die down. So I go over to Sheila and try to make small talk to let her know I'm friendly. I'm not trying to psyche her out. I smile like I did with the other women and try to feel at ease. She looks at me for a fraction of a second before looking down again, answering in a half-syllable. I feel a bit barbed, and back away. *Well if that's the way you want to be believe me I can do that too.*

The contest begins with the women. Feeling divided I join their group again, and we cheer everyone who goes up to the platform. The crowd cheers for each person, gets behind the woman pressing 70 pounds as if it were 503. Except for Sheila. Sheila is still with her trainer in the corner, looking really serious now. I wonder if I should be getting serious and preparing myself instead of standing here clapping for other people.

In the old days I would have. In the old days Sheila would have been me. Something lurches a little in my chest when I look at her face. I remember exactly that look on my face, the not-quite-hostile, guarded skulking, the "just don't mess with me, I'm really serious about this and none of the rest of you frivolous girls are" look that Sheila has at this moment, locking down her brows and pressing together her lips. Seriously warming up. I look at her and move in that direction for a split second, but something in me settles and I turn back to the woman on the platform struggling with 120 and yell out with everyone else, "Go! Go! Come on!" and raise my hands to clap loudly when she racks it up.

In a bench press competition you have three chances to make your highest weight. You open with something you know you can get, then have two more tries to get higher. Right after you get your first press, you have to give the judges the weight of your second attempt. If you miss that weight, you can't go back down again. You can only try to get the same weight or heavier on your third.

In the end Sheila and I have both pressed the same weight, 175. But since she gets all three of her attempts and, trying for 190, I miss two of mine, that means Sheila wins. I swallow and congratulate her. She looks away quickly, mutters "thanks."

I don't accept losing with much grace. I almost leave the meet early because the women's flight goes first, and since there are few of us, goes quickly. There seems no reason to sit through six hours of the men's competition, almost a hundred lifters. I didn't win, won't get a trophy, why stick around? Get me out of this place.

Trying not to seem too disappointed, to cover my shame, I go down to the locker room to change. I start to talk to another lifter, Diane. She just had a baby six weeks ago and is struggling to get back into the gym. The contest, she'd thought, would give her a reason to train, and smiling, flushed, she is really happy with the 120 she'd pressed.

"Every extra pound I get," Diane says, "makes me feel like I'm doing something, you know? Like if I can do this, the rest of my life seems much easier." I know. Looking at it that way, losing one contest doesn't seem like much. My irritation lifts a little.

I understand a few clichés better that day. "Winning isn't everything—it's the only thing" was right up there with "no pain, no gain" when I was running track and cross-country, and I never really thought about the things "winning is the only thing" erased. Just like I used to do, Sheila disappears until it is time to pick up her trophy, telling us clearly she's not part of the crowd. Nope, that's for wussies, for people who aren't any good. But I guess I'm not any good today. I stay. I hang out. I talk to people. I cheer.

Today, for the first time in my life, in the thick of the big rowdy mix of bodies who yell just as loudly for the seventy-five-year-old woman who presses 75 as for the world-record holder who presses 645; the crowd that is on its feet as much for the disabled lifter breaking his personal best of 275 as for the big guys up there in the 500's; the cheers that come just as much for me in my losing attempts as for Sheila, who wins, I feel like I can stand and yell too, part of the scene regardless.

I don't have to win in order to laugh, to talk to people, to take my place. Suddenly I can breathe a little easier, and somewhere in those walls of muscle that make my heart thick, something that's been clenched up really tight for years loosens and falls away. Some ghost within me feels her blood and takes shape. My voice is loud when I shout. In the thick of voices, sweat everywhere, the clang of weights and the smell of chalk, huge guys snorting ammonia and hitting themselves in the head before they run to the bench, throw themselves down, and pop up 600 pounds from their chests, I feel like I belong there, part of the madding crowd. I win no trophy that day. I win some long-dead part of myself instead.

Still, throughout the winter I keep the chest at the forefront of my routine, and six weeks before the next meet hire a trainer to push me further. Heavy negatives, strip sets, practicing my grip. Thinking of Sheila and that 190 I missed, I train so 190 seems easy, and I get my own bench shirt this time. I go into the contest ready to give her a fair run for whatever weight she plans to press, and am a little disappointed when this time she isn't there. "She got burned out or something," one of the guys tells me.

In my stomach something lurches a little, quiet and deep. Boy, had I ever been there. I give blood for Sheila, and Leslie, circa 1984, that day. I get 190, barely miss the 200 I wanted to get. I'll go for 200 again in a couple of weeks, and I'll keep trying until I get it. Maybe after that it'll be 210.

What is it about pushing your body further than it can go that changes your sense of entitlement, your right to be in any space you find yourself? I have watched a father with his daughter, lifting weights. Pushing her like a son. The daughter had on a soccer T-shirt from the Empire State Games, and they were training on the calf machine. Come on, honey, he was saying, just a little harder. Her face strained with the effort and she looked up at him like *I can and I will.* When he goes to her soccer game, will she make him proud? Reflect well on the family name? When she kicks a goal, or makes a save or a really smooth pass to one of her athletic girlfriends, will she feel herself marking the world in that moment, her body moving through the space?

Watching her face, the way she struggled to get the next rep, I knew she would try. Watching them training together, head to head, calf to calf, breath to breath, they were pushing beyond the bounds of their ordinary lives where maybe they are limited, their choices few. But not at this moment. Her straining face, his concentration, father to daughter, arm to arm—in the way she walks, her physical size, her pride, she's getting bigger every day. He's proud of her.

It's been fifteen years since I turned from the track looking for what stood on the other side of my voice and words, for something else to make my heart open, my tendons roar and scream. I didn't have to look far. It's been eighteen years—over half my life—since I first felt iron tear calluses into my skin as I grabbed the gnarled bar in the weight room and hoisted it over my head, growing twelve feet in that second it took to lock my elbows tight. Since I first felt my breath, deep in, help me swing densely iron plates no girl was supposed to lift. Since weights gave me what I needed.

Part of what I needed. The other part is different. After years of training solo, I've got some guys again. But these guys are huge instead of skinny, power lifters not runners, and high school, except for one of us, is years and years behind us. Two of them are married, and I'm part of their group not because they think I'm pretty or because I'm a local star. I'm part of their group because they're generous, and because they know I train hard.

There are three of them, Billy and Chris, who are in their thirties, and Billy's sixteen-year-old son, Jay. I meet them at the gym on Thursday nights, and it's the high point of my week. We start on the bench.

When I first started training with them I was worried, like always, that because I was a girl, they'd automatically move in to spot each other on the heavy weights instead of letting me take my turn. When guys bench together they all take turns spotting, and it shows that each guy is taken seriously and belongs to the group because the lifter is trusting the spotter with his life. He's got to assume that if his muscles fail, his spotter will be strong enough to keep the weight from crashing down on his chest or face.

Most guys let me spot them up to 350 or so, but higher than that they get nervous. I expected the same thing with Billy and Chris. Not a bit. Billy let me spot him without pausing, when I made my move and, preempting Chris, I headed to the back of the bench when the bar had been loaded with 425. I eased up a lot—I smiled more—after that. I'm part of the group, not a tagalong, not the one who's being helped and pushed. In fact, I'm close in strength to Billy and Chris when we lift for our arms, and Jay and I are about the same. It pushes Jay to have me there, and knowing that pushes me too.

On the endurance axis I've got them all beat. But here, the competition is a different thing from anything I've ever done. It really is friendly. We razz each other about cheating on reps—about our butts coming up off the benches when we get tired, about rocking and using our backs when we're doing bicep curls—and though we tease and we push each other, that teasing is part of a support that says each of us feels the other's effort is important, that each of us is important.

It makes me proud to walk across the gym in a pack with these guys, each of us toting our dumbbells to the racks. We are strong, and people often watch us lifting, all four of us, each occupying the end of a bench, joking and doing concentration curls, our biceps clenching all at once. People watch us move together across the floor, and I smile with the joy of being part of these strong ones, these people everyone knows as the ones who train seriously for extraordinary strength. I walk beside them, heavy dumbbells in my hands, my shoulders tight and wide like theirs. This time I am one of the guys in a whole different way that has nothing to do with my hair or my face or anyone's teenage devotional crush. Not that I don't miss very deeply my first set of guys. But I know better this time just what these moments are worth.

How would I feel if these guys were girls? Would I be so comfortable, feel so proud and in place? I don't know. I know I like being the strongest woman in the gym, and get a little nervous if I see anyone who looks like she might compare to me. Nationwide, I've seen one woman in a Kentucky gym who was as strong as me. In California many more than one, and I know New York City has a bunch. I know from the power lifting stats that there are more than twenty women ahead of me in my weight class. How would I feel if I was lifting beside any of these women day to day? Could I feel comfortable with them like I feel with Billy, Chris, and Jay? Would I feel like I really belonged to a pack if I had three other women to train with, women who were stronger than or as strong as me? Stories about female athletes always talk about the sense of camaraderie they feel, and I always wonder if this fellowship is a generational thing, because I know I never had it. I wonder if I didn't because I was in an individual sport, not a team sport, or if it was because of that terrible fierceness in me. Would I be capable of it? Could I go from being one of the guys to being one of the girls? Someday I would like to find out. But I don't think I'm ready just yet.

The immune system attacks don't happen so often now. In the last seven years or so, I've had only a few, always in periods of real stress. Ph.D. orals. Job interviews, divorce, like every so often, those years need to make themselves felt. The last attack—two years ago—came with a high-grade fever for more than two weeks and soaked my sheets for days. I have Raynaud's syndrome, a circulatory disorder where

I lose feeling in my fingers and toes, which turn corpselike blue for lack of blood. I've always appreciated this for its symbolic value.

Sometimes, my joints are stiff, and my elbows ache when I am stacking wood or lifting weights. In spite of the stiffness I still run most days, a slow four-miler with my dog.

I was never a national champion. I remain in memories a big fish in a small pond, one who burned too bright and never made it. But running was the way I first carved myself into the world, how I learned to claim a space, throw my shoulders back, and *fly*. The voices rising, yelling my name as I cruised smoothly by, my legs in perfect motion, taking the track stride by stride: all this has stayed with me, as much a part of me as my prematurely stiff bones or the way my face still turns bloody red whenever I push my heart rate beyond a certain place. The very best of who I was on that track is still who I am every day. And the other stuff? I'll get back to you . . .

R a w   W i n d

I still go back to Tucson every year in July or August. But this summer, the day I stand outside the Amphi track looking in on it, seems a little different. This one marks the fifteenth anniversary from the time I last ran perfect quarters here, from the time I set the state record that still stands. When being a champion, the one who stood out, was my life.

Standing in the dropped heat of Tucson in August, monsoon season, I stare at the track for a while, then turn away from the gap in the chain-link fence and toward the practice fields. I feel tired. There's the football team running over it, the coaches the same, their voices just a little thicker, their faces more deeply cut. Time seems to have stopped here, one set of bodies replaced by the next, the coaches spinning them through like magicians who always stay in the same place.

I turn back to the empty track. How many bodies have run down it since my feet last took its turns? I watch my ghostly shape run around them. I look toward the weight room, under the stadium bleachers. I watch her haunt the weight room eaves. If you went there, you could see me on the sit-up bench, tilted to its furthest height, clenching and heaving through rep after rep, day after day. See me making my intervals in well-timed rings.

Only it wouldn't be me. Girls of flesh and blood have replaced me, and there are more of them, more completely a part of this world now. They travel the weight room in their own packs, and they are not in need of sprinters or coaches to reassure them that they are OK. Watching them, they seem a little stronger than I was, less susceptible to violence and well-timed grief. And that track where I puked and laughed and cried and won belongs to them now.

Once a boyfriend laughed at me and played that Simon & Garfunkel song about being a rock and an island. It was the year my body broke down. The island thing just did not work. I hid behind it, hid behind my races, because I was afraid. Afraid I was nothing, afraid I was too much. Too much anger, too much hate, and never, never enough smiles.

I couldn't reach deep enough to find the place to smile, the place where my breathing was easy and I was visible just because I did breathe. I was just a girl. But I also thought because I won, because I tried so hard, people would see me as someone who counted. So OK, I did count, I did prove myself, but I was left to stutter in my own world, alone and even more afraid. The thing I most needed then has happened now: a whole lot of people have agreed that girls, in fact, do count. I can smile more easily now. Girls in fact do count.

But who knows it? Here I am, back in the same place, and it looks like maybe nothing has changed. I look at the football coaches, yelling and intent to the side of me, the same sets of the shoulders, the same tones cutting up the air above the field I used to hear when I walked here fifteen years ago. Back then, I'm sure they had quite a few stories about me. I don't know whether these stories left a trace or whether everyone has forgotten, like one forgets about a particularly storm-driven spring, what happened exactly, which year it was, which months.

I do know that Coach Luke, wherever he is, is still in me. Sometimes, moving into a set when I'm lifting weights, he is part of my breath, the fierceness and longing that drives me, marks that are part of the raw wind in winter, the stubborn streams that cut through the snow, refusing to freeze. I don't remember what his voice sounded like, only its tone, a velvet claw pressed to the back of my neck, working its way into my mouth. *Ssshhh. Quiet. Sleep, darling, sleep.*

Sometimes I can't sleep and watch *Loveline,* the call-in show with Dr. Drew, addiction medicine specialist, on MTV late night. Some callers have stories like mine—not the same details exactly, but similar motions, touches, words. Like sleepwalkers, they repeat these stories over and over in their lives, the way I've gone through more than several versions of Coach Luke myself.

Who was he? Every so often I wonder. I heard that he went to work for a financial firm after he quit teaching. He married another younger girl a few years after everything happened with me. Did it work out? Was he happy? When he didn't have the sprinters, the football players, the games and the races, what did he do to get what he needed, that feeling of power tight in the chest, the excitement breaking and building in his mouth, *"Let's go, God damn it. Let's see it. Come on, you pussies, drive it out!"?*

Without those daily battles giving his blankness a shape, how did he sleep? What did he do with all the things that had driven him, like all those things that had driven me? And here, on the practice fields to the side of the Amphi track, where their lives had gone on without seeming to change, did they remember him? Did his life leave a trace?

Coach Estes told me once that the thing most inside me, that motivated my running, was hate, and in some ways he was right. Hate kept me going underneath, kept me out of the sadness and then the emptiness where I just shut down. But it's been far too long to keep hating. Standing there, I see myself vanish from that landscape like the shake that erases the Etch a Sketch clean.

I stand very still. What does any of it matter now? Just a story, a ripple on the water long since smoothed, the kind of silence you hear underneath. Everything seems slow. Through the gap in the plastic, I look at the empty track. "Hut-three, hut-four," chime Vern Friedli's kids, the football team, regular as clocks somewhere off to the side. I touch the chain link fence with my forehead. No longer a kid, I hold on.

I'd been to the top of "A" mountain in those years, run faster than any of the guys up the broad face of Kitt Peak, and the rest of my life has seemed like going down the other side, struggling to find another race. After I had to stop running for trophies, the world never quite felt the same. I was not prepared for my diminished place in it. I was not ready to see meaning in simple, daily things. I had seen the Northern Lights, gone flying with the stars.

The adjustment to being human—and just a girl again—was something I've never quite been able to make, like I've been poised in one place, my hand to my ear, waiting to hear the crowd's cheers. Standing here in this stillness, the place where it all went down and then some, I can hear the echoes, mocking me. Real life's not much of a contest. In some ways, at fifteen and sixteen I was most alive, and I've lived expecting my world to turn back to that place where I felt with conviction that I was the sun, some place of magnetic attraction. That illusion was the best I'd get, and it was hard to come down from it. It's why, in the end, no sprinters or coaches could ever take it away: those years were mine.

My years. Years that have surely fled from this place, this deserted track where I stand trespassing in the alley outside. The monsoon rumbles in the background. My fingers tighten a little on the wire of the fence. I still hear the voices cheering me, but the humidity is closing in and I'm starting to sweat. I watch my ghost run down the track. I shake my head. The sound of "hut-three, hut-four" from across the field wipes the echoes out. I can't stay here.

I call out to my ghost, still running, still charging the straights and then floating the curves. I tell her it's OK now.

She can get off the track. She can rest. She smiles, hands on her hips, takes a deep breath, shakes her head, runs off down the track's far lanes. I feel the clench in my stomach let go. One last glance over to Vern and the boys, who never notice me, I don't take her with me when I turn, get into my rental car and drive away.

Epilogue:
One of the Girls

When Gertrude Ederle swam the English Channel in 1926, two hours faster than any of the men who had preceded her, people began to think that women might not be so weak. Imagine her there, her hair cropped short like a flapper, looking into the water and saying *I will*. Imagine the pull of the water that day, the fierceness of the currents, her fearlessness as she greased up. For her, unlike the world that followed her swim, it wasn't a question of whether she could but how fast she would do it. Not wavering a bit, she coats herself from head to foot and heads out. As her face touches water and she takes her first stroke, what she feels is how a wolf feels setting in for an all-day run: she feels right. Her hand passes high above the water with precision and she feels the currents, rolling her over the way they would rough up a boat. Her heart opens with joy, it will be a fight, her muscles pulling the water for hours while exhaustion sets in and she keeps moving. Nothing can stop her, not the manta rays whose tentacles leave a blistering kiss around her throat, not the weather so bad there is an advisory for boats. Twelve hours in, nervous to see the waver in her stroke, the way her arms dip and weave, the way she floats in the seconds in between, her companions pace the deck, lean over the water, cupping their hands in a shout. Gertrude, they say, you should stop. But they're speaking another language, live different lives in which a body doesn't ask itself to dig itself in, to rally, to find an energy that simply doesn't exist, to explode from that gray space of silence and dread into a muscle that is supple, feeling blood beginning to tingle again, ready to bear itself on, to the limit, to the limit, to feel what *is*. No, she says, I have to go.

Forty-one years later, Kathrine Switzer knew she could go the 26.2 miles it took to run the Boston Marathon, knew the feel of the hills and the wind on her skin, knew where she had to dig to scale that inevitable wall, rising at mile 18, when her muscles start to sag and her back is tight far beyond the pounding of her heart stabbing like scabby birch bark. From training runs, she knew the breathing it takes to soar over that wall, the way she had to close her mind to the creeping exhaustion contracting her back, the ache that spreads and spreads like shooting stars of blood rushing through a limb too long compressed, iron spikes between the shoulders. She knew she was up to it. Every day she rose in the morning longing for that ache and the strength that would break in lemon waves, electric. Many times her feet kept moving, still in stride, the air sharp through her lungs past startled pines and leafless maples, through snow and ice, then rain and glittering sleeves of summer green. And every time she scaled that wall and ran beyond those pressing hands along her spine, she opened up. Legs firm and sure, lungs silver-tanked, her strides taking the ground like a monster breathing. *I can do this. Here I am. Watch me run.* And Switzer wants to run like this in an official race, to see it, feel it measured. One for the girls, for the books.

But in 1967, women are not allowed to run. Still she needs to do it. She covers her body and her tracks. She enters the Boston Marathon, K. Switzer, number 261, and goes to the starting line thickened by sweats. A hooded head. No face. The gun goes off and she takes off with the pack, her training partners around her. They start at a decent pace, and breathing, settle in. The hood gathering her face and the top of her head makes her hot. Hothead. Sweat. Two miles in, she pushes it back, her chin-length hair falling free. She looks at her training partner and smiles. Her arms pump, her legs are steady.

But rushing at her from the corner is the race director, midsixties heavy in a long dark coat, stabbing his arms toward the number on her chest. *No girls allowed.* Her partner steps between them, and she pulls away, still running. They leave the race director behind. But then comes another, hips spread wide, rushing at her in heavy boots. Look at his lips curling back from his teeth, *a woman will not compete in this race, not ever, not if it is up to me.* His coat flies up as he grabs at her, his eyes narrowed to a slit. Her partner rushes between them again as Kathrine turns and slips away. For 24.2 more miles. Her heart beats even heavier, adrenaline strong. *I will do this.*

And this time there is no wall rising at mile 18. This time, the four hours and twenty minutes it takes her to finish are a lime-long breeze. Pain in her ankles, ball joints of her hips, steel clamps on her neck, she breathes easy. Heart steadier than ever. When the newspapers mob the race director and ask him to speak, he says that he is "hurt to think that an American girl would go where she is not wanted. If that girl were my daughter I would spank her." So they turn to Switzer. Ask her why she runs. Because running makes her "strong, all there." It is another five years, 1972, before women are allowed to run, pound out the long roads laid by the still-grown trees. Stronger than strong. All there. They come. They run.

This is where I begin. Title IX of the Education Act of 1972, that law that made gender discrimination illegal, made athletes of millions of girls like me. No more female incompetence and physical weakness, *you throw like a girl, no girls allowed, why don't you just go home.* Not now, excuse me. Stepping out.

So now she is everywhere around us, staring back at you from the television screen, from women's magazines: a fierce babe with biceps, straight shoulders, a proud look, claiming the planet for her own. Gabby Reece. Lisa Leslie. Rebecca Lobo. Mia Hamm. She's given to us in blacks and in whites: you can see the stark beauty of her body like straight-line cords. She's no one you would mess with. She's someone you might like to become. She's beautiful. She's strong. She's proud. She's doing it for herself: you project on her all the strength you've never felt, all the invulnerability you've never mustered, all the desire for self-sufficiency and completion you've never owned. She has it. You want it. Look closer.

Are you the one she's looking at when she asks if you'll let her play sports? Are you the one who'll prepare her to win? Are you the one who follows, looks, watches her step out and stride? If she lets you touch her, is it because she wants to be touched? What if she turned from her chiseled silhouette, poised, and looked you in the face? What if she could speak? What if she could tell you a story you haven't heard, not yet, what if the image of perfection took on some blood and began to tell you? Would you listen? Would you follow her voice like a glistening chime? Would her story take you over, overcome where you need her to stay—way up there pedestaled, just out of reach, an image of hope and a goal that you can become— sometime soon, next month or next week? But who is she? How does she live? What does she think about, what does she eat? Who touches her, who does she touch? Her muscles, her body, her pillars of strength—what's inside her? Is her life like yours, like your best friend's? Look closer.

There are some great Nike ads out there that are a gateway to my vanished world, where I used to win races and everyone knew. In the black-and-white images, dreams, possibilities beckon to girls, welcome them into the world. Sports can give us that place, but a lot of work needs to be done before we've finished that race. Female athletes fight the same unrealistic images everyone fights, and researchers are only beginning to understand the relationship between those images and the "female athlete triad"—eating disorders and exercise compulsion, amenorrhea—that had me training until my bones fractured, my tendons ripped, and I stuck my fingers down my throat or simply didn't eat to stay lean. Nobody's been quite loud enough in saying that the female athlete triad is almost surely connected to all the old negative ideas about girls—girls trying to prove beyond a shadow of a doubt that they are not what those ideas say they are: weak, mild, meek, meant to serve others instead of achieving for themselves. The ideas that made the race directors chase Kathrine Switzer away.

Are those ideas really gone? Let's face it—many of the images of female athletes out there are more about having a great butt or a great set of pecs than they are about winning races and feeling confident. If we really want a society where, as one of the young girls in the Nike ads says, "I can be anything I want to be," each of us will have to do everything we can to make this dream more than words sliding easily out of the mouth. We need to make sure Title IX is enforced so that as many girls as possible have the opportunity to play sports. We need to make sure girls are treated as athletes, not just pretty girls. We need to continue the research that's been started on all the different aspects of girls' and women's lives, which shows sports' potential to give us a sense of competence and power—like that feeling deep in my lungs as, running by, I dared the very cacti not to see me.

Because national attention has turned to female athletes, because we are no longer disparaged or scorned, or seen as exceptions to the woman-as-weakness rule, I know some things now I didn't know then. I belonged to the first wave of women in sports after Title IX, part of the gathering wave that ballooned the stats from 300,000 girls in interscholastic athletics to the 2.25 million who play today. Is it really safe now? Can we begin to try out some of the new ideas about competing, ideas I was struggling with competing against Sheila in the gym? Can we smile at each other without being fake? Can we find ways to get out there, still swallowing the world, still roaring like Tarzan swinging mightily on his vines, and not have to knock everyone else off the vines just so it looks like we're the one who soars best? Can we move toward what, in her new book, *Embracing Victory,* Mariah Burton Nelson names "the Champion" model of competition, which "respects all contestants, including the self"?

The old competitive model—what I did—led many of us from an earlier generation to the female athlete triad, and we missed out on the true benefits of sports. Can we revise people's ideas about girls enough so that my ghost will give up having to prove herself, and the other girls running in her place won't have to erase whole worlds inside themselves just so someone will notice them, just so they can stand out and win?

In spite of everything that happened I continued in sport. I knew instinctively what research is proving now: sports, if not played in the way I did, where everyone around you had to be stomped out with boots to their face because there was only one winner and it had to be you—if played a little differently than this, sports help with depression. They help with what the books call self-esteem: feeling the sun on your warm face, walking across the field like a giant, feeling that just for a moment, the world belongs to you.

Running and lifting are as much a part of my life as is the quiet in-and-out of my steady chest. I write this book with hopes that other girls will have some support I didn't have and won't make the same mistakes. So here's to many, many more women's hockey teams and Picabo Streets—and to the women and men who'll work hard to make it possible for every young girl to burn bright as the sun without paying the price of self-destruction. And then when there are girls all around who are stronger and with better biceps than me, well, I just might be able to deal with it.

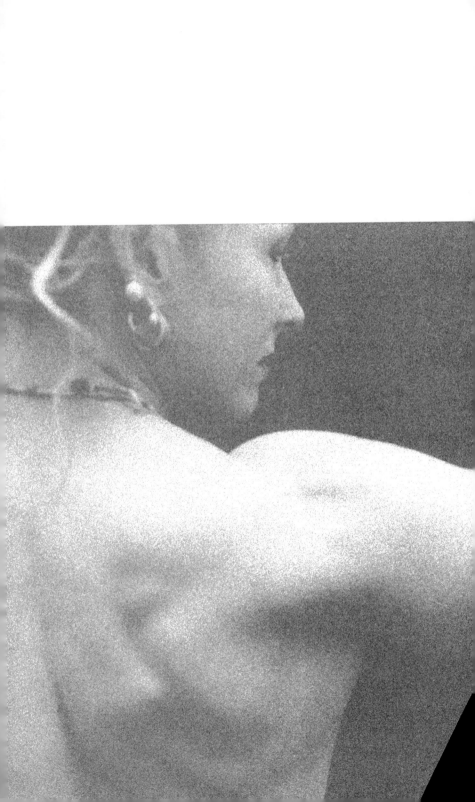

Leslie Heywood is assistant professor in the English Department at the State University of New York, Binghamton, where she teaches cultural studies, feminist theory, and twentieth-century literature. She has a Ph.D. from the University of California, Irvine, and an M.F.A. in poetry from the University of Arizona. A former University of Arizona track star and cross-country runner, and a current power lifter and bodybuilder, Heywood's work focuses on issues of the body, gender, and image in contemporary American culture. She is the author of *Dedication to Hunger: The Anorexic Aesthetic in Modern Culture*, *Bodymakers: A Cultural Anatomy of Women's Bodybuilding*, and co-editor, with Jennifer Drake, of *Third Wave Agenda: Being Feminist, Doing Feminism* (University of Minnesota Press).